Praise for
Field Marshal Montgomery's Professionalism and Its Effects on Allied Campaigns

"Generals are notorious for exaggerating battlefield success and for fudging the facts when the facts are unflattering. Paul Teague demonstrates that Field Marshal Sir Bernard Montgomery, arguably one of World War II's most competent and, effective allied commanders, was no exception to this rule. Teague tells a revealing story that will concentrate the minds of students and practitioners of the military art on the pitfalls of high command in war."

—**DOUGLAS MACGREGOR**, Colonel (ret) U.S. Army. Author of *Margin of Victory: Five Battles that Changed the Face of Modern War*

FIELD MARSHAL MONTGOMERY'S

PROFESSIONALISM

AND ITS EFFECTS ON

ALLIED CAMPAIGNS

Paul S. Teague, Major, United States Army Retired

VIRGINIA BEACH
CAPE CHARLES

*Field Marshal Montgomery's
Professionalism and Its Effects
on Allied Campaigns*

by *Paul S. Teague, Major, United States Army Retired*

© Copyright 2018 Paul S. Teague

ISBN 978-1-63393-713-0

All rights reserved. No part of this publication may be reproduced, stored in a retrieval system, or transmitted in any form or by any means—electronic, mechanical, photocopy, recording, or any other—except for brief quotations in printed reviews, without the prior written permission of the author.

Cover image found on Wiki Commons. This work is greated by the United Kingdom Government is in the public domain.

Published by

köehlerbooks™

210 60th Street
Virginia Beach, VA 23451
212-574-7939
www.koehlerbooks.com

DEDICATION

To my beloved wife, Kabaka Mutesa Teague, Master Sergeant, United States Army Reserve (Retired), the mother of my three children, Kendra, Isabelle, and Paul. She is the reason I am able to "Charlie Mike."

AUTHOR'S NOTE

Historians seem to have divided themselves into pro-Montgomery or anti-Montgomery cliques. The pro-Montgomery historians find no fault in him; the anti-Montgomery historians find no virtues. Not wishing to be included in either group, I have made a concerted effort to be fair in my analysis of the historical evidence concerning Montgomery during the Second World War. Though most of my conclusions may seem harsh, I am confident that I did give credit where credit is due. Montgomery's generalship at Alam Haifa and Second Alamein was dynamic and decisive. It is safe to say no general, British or American, would have done better. His modifications to the Overlord plan ensured success on that crucial day, June 6, 1944. Without Montgomery, D-Day could have been a disastrous defeat; instead, it was a magnificent victory.

FOREWORD

This excellent book focuses on the strengths and weaknesses of a legendary military leader from World War II, Field Marshal Bernard Law Montgomery. All great leaders, military or civilian, are first and foremost individuals with unique personalities. In this volume, Paul Teague excels in sharing with the reader an analysis of Field Marshal Montgomery's many strengths, his notable weaknesses, and how those strengths and weaknesses affected Allied campaigns during the conflict. After a discussion of Bernard Law Montgomery's formative early years and how they influenced both his strengths and his weaknesses, Paul Teague recounts Montgomery's tactical and operational activities in North Africa, Sicily, Italy, the invasion of France at Normandy, and the Allied march toward Berlin.

Any successful study of military leadership includes many perspectives. As you read through this work, be alert to how Paul addresses Field Marshal Montgomery's interactions with both his military and his civilian counterparts and superiors (civil-military relations), and how Montgomery attempted to use and manipulate the media to his and the Allies' advantage (military-media relations). You will learn about how Montgomery handled dissent and ethical issues, both his own and those of others. One of the fundamental responsibilities of any leader is to identify and prepare those who will one day replace you. Paul shows us how Montgomery approached that responsibility throughout his career.

As noted before, each leader is first and foremost an individual with a unique personality.

Paul Teague relates that there are three tenets of British military professionalism; approach, study, and followership. He then notes that the six core values of the British Army relate very closely to military professionalism. They are selfless commitment, courage, discipline, integrity, loyalty, and respect for others. The author clearly illustrates where Field Marshal Montgomery met those standards and where he did not.

Montgomery was known for his very impressive ego, but his was not the only massive one among Allied leaders or their adversaries. The author explores the interaction among those egos, and how those interactions affected Allied operations, both positively and negatively. Montgomery was consumed by his need to be perceived not only as successful but as the most successful commander of his time. It is interesting to see how the Montgomery ego influenced his relationships with his less egocentric military and civilian superiors.

In the almost three decades since my retirement, I have had opportunities to teach about strategic leadership and joint warfare for the Naval War College, the Naval Postgraduate School, and the American Military University. As part-time faculty with the American Military University for many years, I had the good fortune to have Paul Teague as a participant in the courses I taught related to joint warfare's theory and practice; joint warfare's command and control; and strategic military leadership. In each, Paul received an A and the highest numerical grade among his classmates. Paul Teague is intellectually curious, insightful, and an outstanding writer. That will become very evident as you read through his work. I am honored that Paul asked me to provide this foreword to his book.

    Richard B. Goetze,
    Jr. Ph.D. Major General, USAF (retired)

TABLE OF CONTENTS

Author's Note VII
Foreword... IX
Preface XV
Chapter I: Introduction 1
Chapter II: Background 4
Chapter III: North Africa...21
Chapter IV: Sicily... 55
Chapter V: Italy 70
Chapter VI: Normandy 78
Chapter VII: Antwerp 101
Chapter VIII: Operation Market Garden 116
Chapter IX: Ardennes Offensive................................ 128
Chapter X: Crossing the Rhine River........................ 140
Chapter XI: Command Structure................................147
Chapter XII: Conclusion 156
APPENDIX 1: The Literature......................................166
APPENDIX 2: Significant Dates.................................178
APPENDIX 3: Comparative Officer Ranks 183
APPENDIX 4: Comparative Commands 184
APPENDIX 5: Maps 186
Bibliography 201
Acknowledgments... 210

PREFACE

Historians generally agree that Field Marshal Bernard Law Montgomery enjoyed the reputation as perhaps the most competent and professional Allied commander of the Second World War. They also agree he was an egotist: tactless, divisive, and arrogant. These characteristics not only affected his generalship but are in complete contrast to the British Army's tenets of professionalism. To be sure, other commanders exhibited these characteristics: George Patton certainly did on occasion, as did Erwin Rommel. However, command constraints on Montgomery were less restrictive than on the others. Historians accurately describe Montgomery's battlefield setbacks but fail to include his negative characteristics in their analysis of his generalship that shaped the conditions for these setbacks. Historians considered pro-Montgomery typically lay the blame at the feet of Montgomery's superiors or subordinates, while others cast all the blame on his overcautiousness. At Alam Halfa and Second Alamein, Montgomery demonstrated he could be flexible and decisive in winning a defensive battle. It was after he gained these victories, and thus gained opportunities to counterattack, that he showed a lack of aggressiveness. When the time came for decisive flexibility in the offense, Montgomery faltered. After all, he had to protect the newly won gains to his reputation at Second Alamein. By analyzing Montgomery within the framework of British Army tenets, one can make a more accurate assessment of his professionalism and its effects upon his generalship and upon Allied operations.

CHAPTER I:
INTRODUCTION

Historians have been quite frank in identifying Montgomery's flaws in generalship during the conduct of his campaigns, yet they still regard him as one of the most professional and competent Allied commanders. How can this be? How is it that Montgomery failed to destroy Army Group Africa after the Battle of Alam Halfa when he possessed superiority in every category of combat power? How did Army Group Africa evade destruction after the battle of Second Alamein, when Montgomery's advantage was even greater than at Alam Halfa? How did the remnants of Army Group Africa, low on ammunition and fuel, conduct successful retrograde operations against Montgomery's pursuing forces for six months across North Africa? What were the flaws in Montgomery's ground plan for Sicily that failed to prevent German retreat from the island? What were the causes of Montgomery's slow advance to reinforce the Allied landings at Salerno, Italy? What were the reasons for Montgomery's failure to open the Port of Antwerp in a timely fashion? What caused Montgomery, the cautious and detailed planner, to launch the disastrous Operation Market Garden, history's largest airborne operation, only ten days after planning began?

This work will analyze Field Marshal Montgomery's performance of duty during World War Two. Its focus will be his generalship during critical events in the war, to determine if his decisions were based on operational and tactical considerations or motivated by personal ones. These events will include his planning of the Dieppe Raid in 1942, his North African Campaign in 1942 to 1943, his campaigns in Sicily and Italy in 1943, and the northern Europe Campaign in 1944 to 1945. Also critical to the analysis is the state of his relationships with personalities such as General Dwight Eisenhower, Field Marshal Alan Brooke, General Omar Bradley, General Claude Auchinleck, and Field Marshal Harold Alexander.

Montgomery's first battle in North Africa, at Alam Halfa, demonstrated that despite what many historians have written, he possessed the attributes of flexibility and decisiveness. His next, more famous battle, Second Alamein, made his reputation. He again showed flexibility and decisiveness in breaking out his Eighth Army and forcing Panzer Group Africa to retreat. However, after achieving this great victory, rather than take the opportunity to destroy Rommel's Panzer Army Africa, Montgomery hesitated. His flexibility and decisiveness seemed to escape him, allowing the enemy to withdraw. Montgomery was a student of history, and he knew he had won a victory of historical significance. However, he did not wish to execute an immediate pursuit, as tactical expediency required, and risk tarnishing his achievement. After Second Alamein, Montgomery resembled the classical Greek generals who let the defeated depart the field, rather than Alexander, who pursued the enemy immediately and relentlessly after a victory. However, one has to remember that Montgomery also had concerns about his soldiers' training level of at that time. Perhaps he thought conservation of his forces was the more prudent course.[1]

By examining Montgomery's well-documented personality and his military activities through the British Army's tenets of professionalism and six core values, one can make a more accurate assessment of his reputation as the most professional and competent Allied commander of World War Two. A study of his professional relationships with superiors and peers will reveal Montgomery's efforts to maintain the reputation he gained at Second Alamein degraded Allied unity of effort, hurt military operations, and may have prolonged the war.

The work relies on primary sources consisting of texts by those who commanded Montgomery, served alongside him, and served under him, as well as writings by Montgomery and published documents. Secondary sources contributing to this study are works published by academic and military historians since the end of the war. Also included as sources are the writings of Montgomery's official biographer Nigel Hamilton, as are the texts of journalists who covered the war.

---

[1] J. K. Anderson, *Military Theory and Practice in the Age of Xenophon* (Berkeley: University of California Press, 1970), 190.

CHAPTER II:
BACKGROUND

Bernard Law Montgomery was born in Kennington on the outskirts of London on November 17, 1887. His father, Reverend Henry Montgomery, was vicar of Saint Mark's of Kennington. His mother, Maud, who married Henry when she was sixteen, was the perfect vicar's wife, supportive of her husband and a strict disciplinarian to their children. Maude bore her husband five children, Sibyl, Harold, Donald, Bernard, and Una.[2]

Maud, who became overbearing, took complete control of the household, regulating even the vicar to a secondary role in the home. The children respected their mother but held little affection for her, and Maud rarely displayed any for them. Indeed, if any child was guilty of an infraction of the many rules Maude set for them, they were beaten. The children loved their father, though he was often away from home on church business.

---

[2] Nigel Hamilton, *Monty: The Making of a General 1887-1942* (New York: McGraw-Hill, 1981). 2-3

Maud demonstrated her complete dominance in how she took her daily naps. Only the vicar was allowed in the house while Maud rested for two hours every afternoon. The children had to make do outside, regardless of the weather. On no account was Maude to be disturbed.[3] Montgomery adopted a similar practice years later in North Africa while in command of the British Eighth Army. Upon completing dinner, Montgomery would retire for the evening evoking his own ironclad rule that he was not, for any reason, to be disturbed regardless of the situation.[4]

Montgomery's brothers and sisters escaped from the dictatorial clutches of Maud and their loveless home as soon as they could. Harold departed for Africa as soon as he was of age; Donald escaped to Canada where he became a successful lawyer, Una married and went to Egypt with her husband. Unfortunately, Sibyl died in her youth. Bernard was not yet old enough to leave home, and this left Bernard to the mercies of Maud. Bernard was not only the black sheep of the family, but he was now the only sheep. For the next few years, he would engage in a war of wills with his mother. He took every opportunity to impose his will on himself as well as others while Maud continued her efforts to bend Bernard to her will. This unhappy home life embittered young Montgomery, and it had a profound effect on his life and his relations with others.[5]

Later in life, he blamed his mother's lack of affection and unattainable standards for the unbending strict discipline he would come to inflict on others. All of Bernard's affection went toward his father; however, the affection he reserved for his mother was never displayed because she never returned it. As a result, he learned to keep his affections, as well as his other

---

3 Ibid., 34.
4 Francis De Guingand, *Operation Victory* (London: Hodder and Stoughton, 1947), 193.
5 Viscount of Alamein Montgomery, *Memoirs, Montgomery of Alamein* (Cleveland: World Publishing Company, 1958), 17.

emotions, bottled up within himself.[6] This habit would remain with him for the rest of his life. As a result, Montgomery was determined to escape from his oppressive home.[7]

Bernard received some relief when he was enrolled in St. Paul's school in London at the age of fourteen. On his first day there he signed up the Army class, much to the dismay of his parents. The Army program at St. Paul's did not necessarily mean Bernard would find himself in the Army, but it was an option for his eventual escape from his mother.[8]

While at St Paul's, Montgomery proved a below average student; however, he discovered he had talent as an athlete. Though not impressive in size, he possessed a determination to succeed on the playing fields that brought him a sense of accomplishment. Perhaps for the first time in his life, he felt the exhilaration of being looked up to by his teammates and the other students. Here at St. Paul's, he may have felt not only that he could escape from his mother but perhaps that he could even make her proud of him and at last show some affection for him.[9] Alas, this was not to be. His accomplishment in sports would be overshadowed, in his parents' eyes, by his lack of academic achievement.

Though not strong academically, Montgomery did well enough on the entrance examinations to gain acceptance into Sandhurst in January 1907. Initially, he thrived at the academy, and after only five weeks he was promoted to Lance-Corporal and was becoming a standout on the hockey and rugby teams. Montgomery was nineteen years old, finally away from his overbearing mother, and beginning to realize that his upbringing of strict discipline, lack of affection, self-reliance, and lack of

---

6   Hamilton, *Monty: The Making of a General*, 5-6.
7   Montgomery, *Memoirs*, 18.
8   Hamilton, *Monty: The Making of a General*, 42.
9   Montgomery, *Memoirs*, 20-21.

consideration of others were now a part of him. This gave him a sense of superiority and was making him a leader among his peers. Indeed, even the company he was assigned to, B Company, gained a reputation for fighting amongst themselves and other companies. The young men in B Company seemed to revel in cruelty, and Montgomery was looked upon as their leader.

This thuglike activity reached a crisis in December 1907, when Montgomery led some members of his company in an attack on another cadet whom Montgomery did not like. The unfortunate cadet was in the process of dressing when Montgomery's gang held him down and Montgomery set the victim's shirttail on fire. The cadet was badly burned and required hospitalization; however, his sense of honor would not let him tell the authorities who had set him on fire. The cadre at Sandhurst soon discovered that Montgomery was the culprit, and when he was confronted with the deed, he admitted to it. Though he feared expulsion, his punishment was reduction to the lowest cadet rank. He was, however, allowed to continue his studies and eventually gain his commission. Not surprisingly, Montgomery was labeled a maladjusted young man.[10]

On September 19, 1908, Montgomery received his commission as Lieutenant in the Royal Warwickshire Regiment and set out for to the Northwest Frontier of India. He would remain in India until his battalion was transferred back to England in 1913 on the eve of the First World War. During his time in India, Montgomery developed two more characteristics he would consistently display in his later career. First, he came to love the British soldier, who was always willing to carry on despite the shortcomings of their leaders. Second, he came to disdain his peers and superiors whom he felt did not measure up to his perceived ideas of professionalism. Those officers

---

10 Hamilton, *Monty: The Making of a General*, 48-49.

who did not study their profession and were perfectly content to serve their time at battalion level became anathema to him.[11] This attitude, developed in India, may provide some insight into Montgomery's subsequent care of his soldiers as well as his inability to get along with peers and superiors.

While back in England, Montgomery met an officer from another battalion within the regiment named Captain Lefroy. Lefroy held many of the same opinions as Montgomery, and a strong friendship developed. Montgomery looked up to Lefroy as a mentor. They had long discussions on soldiering, leadership, and warfare, Montgomery listened to Lefroy's every word. The friendship lasted until Lefroy's death in 1915. It had a profound effect on Montgomery who would later write about his experience with Captain Lefroy, "It is important for a young officer to come in contact with the best type of officer and the right influences early in his military career."[12] Surely, it was Montgomery's memory of his mentorship by Captain Lefroy that led him to become a caring mentor and role model to his many young staff officers during his various command assignments.

When the First World War broke out, Montgomery went to France with his regiment and found himself commanding a platoon as a full Lieutenant on the western front. At this stage in his career, he was already demonstrating what many would later refer to as a high degree of professionalism. An incident during the war best illustrates this. Montgomery's regiment was defending in Méteren, near the French border with Belgium. Regulations at the time dictated that commanders in the defense should examine their positions from the enemy viewpoint. So he walked out into no man's land and turned his back upon the enemy to see through their eyes. While doing so, he was shot in the back by a German sniper. The bullet tore through his

---

11 Montgomery, *Memoirs*, 28-29.
12 Ibid., 31.

lung, collapsing it. One of his soldiers rushed out to save him. As the soldier was applying a field dressing, the sniper shot him through the head, killing him. After nightfall, Montgomery's troops retrieved him. While this act showed courage and knowledge of the regulations, it also demonstrated, to anyone who has been in combat, a lack of judgment. Even allowing for Montgomery's youth at twenty-six, he did already have combat experience during the retreat from Mons and fighting on the Aisne, enough to know better. Montgomery would be evacuated back to England to recuperate. When he was well enough to return to France, he finished the war serving in staff positions.[13]

During the inter-war years, Montgomery commanded a company and attended the Staff College at Camberley in 1922. In 1923, while serving on the staff of the 49th Division, he began writing the doctrine for the updated *British Army Infantry Manual*. For all that has been written about Montgomery's study of war (the first mark of a professional soldier), he did not understand exploitation. This is key to understanding Montgomery and the effect on his campaigns, for it is exploitation that brings decisive victory. In 1924, Montgomery wrote several training pamphlets and sent them to his friend B.H. Liddell Hart for a review. Montgomery had great respect for Liddell Hart and thought he was a critical thinker, the type of officer that was missing at the staff college.

The other great British military theorist, General J.F.C. Fuller, was at this time deeply involved in his pursuit of interest in the occult and correspondence with the occultist Aleister Crowley. In 1923, he wrote an article, "The Black Arts" for *The Occult Review,* and the next year had a book, *Yoga,* published. It is little wonder Montgomery did not request Fuller's views on his doctrinal writings.

---

13 Montgomery, *Memoirs,* 33.; Hamilton, *The Making of a General* 88.

Liddell Hart expressed surprise that Montgomery had neglected to discuss the need for exploiting success on the battlefield. In 1931, Montgomery drafted a new Army Manual on the attack and the defense. Again he sent the draft to Liddell Hart for comment. Liddell Hart's critique again mentioned this lack of focus and included the information Montgomery was missing on exploitation in maneuvering. When the Manual was published in 1932, Liddell Hart found that Montgomery had still not adequately addressed the subject. He later wrote that Montgomery's failure to understand exploitation was evident in the Second Battle of Alamein and subsequent battles, where he repeatedly missed the opportunity the breakout created, letting the enemy slip away to fight another day.[14]

In 1931, Montgomery was promoted to Lieutenant Colonel. He does not write much in his memoirs about the period between 1931 and 1934, when he had his command of the 1st Battalion, Royal Warwickshire Regiment. The reason for this is that his battalion command was hardly a success. According to Dr. Norman Dixon, Montgomery commanded with a harsh self-righteousness, used too firm a grip, and used it tactlessly. This degraded the morale and cohesiveness of the battalion. Indeed, Colonel Pat Burge, who commanded a platoon in Montgomery's Battalion, confirmed that regimental confidence and ceremonial pride suffered a great blow when Montgomery took over command in January 1931.[15]

While still in Egypt, Montgomery pressured his company commanders to alter marksmanship scores to reflect an extremely high number of First-Class Marksmen to make his battalion look better. Afterward, it transferred to India where, soon after, Montgomery left command. A few days later the 1st went to the

---

14 Hamilton, *The Making of a General* 88.
15 Dr. Norman Dixon, *On the Psychology of Military Incompetence* (London: Futura Publications, 1985), 357.; Hamilton, *Monty: The Making of a General*, 217.

firing range where not one soldier was able to score better than Third-Class Marksman. A scandal resulted, but Montgomery had already departed command. As a result, he did not have to answer for this lack of integrity upon his return to England.[16]

Back in England, Montgomery took command of the 9th Infantry Brigade in June 1937 at Portsmouth and advanced to the temporary grade of Brigadier General. Sadly, a few months later, his wife Betty died. The following year Montgomery was posted to Palestine, where he took over command of the 8th Division in Haifa. With this assignment came promotion to Major General. Montgomery participated in quelling the Arab revolt in the winter of 1938 to 1939. In the spring of 1939, Montgomery became very ill and was evacuated back to England. When he was well enough to return to Palestine, he was informed that he was to take command of the 3rd Division in England.[17]

In the early morning of September 1, 1939, the armed forces of Hitler's Germany invaded Poland, beginning the Second World War. Two days later, Great Britain, which had signed a Mutual Defense Agreement with Poland in March 1939, declared war on Germany. Upon the outbreak of the war, Montgomery was a Major General commanding the British 3rd Division. The 3rd Division was assigned to the II Corps of the 1st British Expeditionary Force, commanded by Lieutenant General Alanbrooke. Montgomery, Alanbrooke, and Major General Harold Alexander, who commanded the 1st Division of the I Corps, would be linked together throughout the war. Montgomery's relationships with Alanbrooke and Alexander are critical to the analysis of his professionalism and generalship.[18]

Montgomery had trained the 3rd Division to a high level of competence, and it was with confidence that he led the Division

---

[16] Hamilton, *Monty: The Making of a General*, 243.
[17] Montgomery of Alamein, *Memoirs*, 42-45.
[18] Ibid., 123.

against the German onslaught in Belgium and France. Although the division did not decisively engage with the Germans, Montgomery showed great skill in withdrawing it to Dunkirk. Both Corps commanders, Lieutenant General Barker of I Corps and Lieutenant General Brooke, were recalled to England, leaving Alexander in command of I Corps and Montgomery in command of II Corps. Montgomery evacuated II Corps on May 31, 1940, and Alexander followed with I Corps a few days later. The evacuation of the British and French forces from Dunkirk took nine days, with 338,000 soldiers escaping death or captivity. However, the British army had lost in battle, and so much equipment had been left in France that Montgomery's division was the only fully equipped division in England.[19]

Back in England, Montgomery asked to take command of the 3rd Division once more, and permission was granted. Montgomery was directed to ready his division for movement back to France not later than mid-June, as his was the only fully equipped division left in England. To prepare for this mission, he canceled all leaves. This was a severe blow to the soldiers of his division, who were expecting the same leave the other returning divisions had received. They just wanted to show their families they were still alive and well. The troops took it very badly, and morale suffered. Montgomery's primary concern was operational security; he was not willing to risk one of his soldiers telling a family member about any of the division's upcoming deployments.[20]

The return to France never took place, as it capitulated on June 17. The 3rd Division then deployed to the southern coast as part of the defense of England. In July 1942, Montgomery was promoted to Lieutenant General and took command of V Corps,

---

19   Montgomery of Alamein, *A History of Warfare* (New York: William Morrow, 1983), 502.
20   Montgomery of Alamein, *Memoirs*, 59-63.; Hamilton, *Monty: The Making of a General*, 400.

which would defend Hampshire and Dorset. V Corps was part of the South East Command with General Claude Auchinleck as commander. Montgomery's relations with Auchinleck were strained, as Montgomery felt he had more combat experience and military knowledge than Auchinleck. Their discomfort with each other remained until December 1941, when Auchinleck left to become Commander-in-Chief of the Middle East. Montgomery later wrote in his memoirs, "I cannot recall that we ever agreed on anything."[21]

Montgomery subsequently took command of South East Command. On his own and without authorization, he changed its name to the South East Army and declared himself an Army commander. One is reminded of Major General Patton pinning the three stars of a Lieutenant General on his collar before his official promotion to that grade, upon assuming command of the U.S. II Corps in North Africa.[22]

As the South East commander, Montgomery planned ground operations and allocated the 2nd Canadian Division for the raid on Dieppe. The mission was under the overall command of Admiral Lord Mountbatten. It was intended to gain knowledge of German capabilities on the French coast and to test Allied amphibious techniques. Its original plan called for the main assaults to go in on the flanks, using what was then known as the indirect approach. However, Montgomery began a habit he would continue throughout the war: changing the plan to suit himself. He rejected the "flanks only" plan and directed a frontal attack instead. He insisted this would be successful if a massive aerial bombardment were available to neutralize German defenses in and around Dieppe. On June 5, 1942, the RAF notified Montgomery that an aerial bombardment would not be

---

21   Ibid., 65.
22   Ibid., 63-65.

possible for the raid, as the aircraft would be attacking higher priority targets in Germany. Montgomery reluctantly agreed to abandon the bombing of Dieppe. However, he recommended the direct frontal attack go forward as planned. The raid was scheduled for July 4, 1942, but was delayed because of weather.[23]

Montgomery considered the plan for the raid now moot. However, when Mountbatten revived the scheme and set August 19 as the date of execution, Montgomery was both surprised and upset. He left England on August 10 to take command of the Eighth Army in Egypt. The raid was an unmitigated disaster. Admiral Lord Mountbatten, as the overall commander and driving force behind the operation, was responsible for the failure. The Allies lost all their equipment and suffered 3,369 casualties, 907 of which were killed in action. These are staggering numbers when one considers that the total raiding force was 5,000 men.[24]

Montgomery spent much time and effort trying to separate himself from the disaster at Dieppe. After all, he was not the responsible commander, and he had recommended permanently canceling the operation. However, it was his ground plan that was carried out, and as a professional officer, he should have accepted his portion of responsibility for the defeat. Subsequent successes would overshadow his central role in planning the dreadful raid on Dieppe. Montgomery would later state, "I believe we could have got the information and experience we needed without losing so many magnificent Canadian soldiers." [25]That had not been his opinion when he had insisted on a suicidal frontal attack on the beaches of Dieppe. However, he later put the lessons learned from the raid to excellent use when he planned the Allied landings as part of Operation Overlord in 1944.

---

23   Terence Robertson, *Dieppe: The Shame and the Glory* (Boston: Little, Brown and Company, 1962), 95-96.
24   Montgomery of Alamein, *Memoirs*, 70-71.
25   Ibid., 71.

While Montgomery had South East Command, his former commander, General Auchinleck, who took over Middle East Command in July 1941, was fighting Rommel's Panzer Army Africa in a series of seesaw battles. The British did have some success in the desert war. On December 8, 1940, the Western Task Force, then under the command of Major General Richard O'Conner attacked toward Tobruk, culminating with its capture on January 22, 1941. By February 8, the force had taken Mersa Brega and Agheila. With only two divisions, O'Conner had defeated ten Italian divisions, capturing 130,000 Italians, 380 armored vehicles, and 845 guns. O'Conner lost 500 killed and 1,400 wounded. It was one of the most successful Allied operations of the war.

However, since then, the Germans had come to the aid of the Italians. As the situation worsened, Auchinleck took command of the Eighth Army. Panzer Army Africa contained the famed Afrika Korps, the German 90th Light Division, and three Italian Corps, the X, XX, and XXI. The German assessment of the Italian combat capabilities was dismal. On February 1, 1941, General Funck, a General Staff Officer returned from Libya, briefed Hitler on the capabilities of the Italians in North Africa. He claimed they were so poor as to verge on sabotage.[26]

By July 1942, Rommel had advanced to El Alamein, about sixty miles west of Alexandria. It was here that the tide of the war in Africa would turn, in what became known as the Battle of First Alamein. In choosing the area south of El Alamein to defend, Auchinleck showed his generalship. This battle was his first and last as the Eighth Army commander, and he was indeed up to it. He exploited the area's terrain well: using the sea on his right and the Qattara Depression, where no armored vehicles

---

26 Montgomery of Alamein, *A History of Warfare*, 506-507.; Gerhard Engle, *At the Heart of the Reich: The Secret Diary of Hitler's Army Adjutant* tr. Geoffrey Brooke (London: Greenhill Books, 2005), 103.

could maneuver, on his left, he would canalize Rommel's forces into his center and force the Germans to execute the least favored form of offensive maneuver, the frontal attack. This would make it easy for him to pound the Germans with close air support and massed artillery fire. Auchinleck also reinforced his defense with a plethora of minefields.[27]

Rommel attacked into Auchinleck's superb defensive scheme on July 1, 1942. Each time Rommel thought he had found an opening, Auchinleck was able to close it by deploying his mobile reserve forces to counterattack and repulse the Germans. For over two weeks, Rommel tried to defeat Auchinleck's defense but had no success, as the Eighth Army turned back one attack after another. By September 17, morale in the Afrika Korps had sunk so low that the Italian Trento Division surrendered to the Eighth Army. Over the next two weeks, the situation continued to decline.

By July 30, Rommel knew he had been beaten. Auchinleck had outfoxed the Desert Fox. Rommel described the First Battle of Alamein as militarily the most difficult period he had ever been through, and he regarded Auchinleck's Generalship as an "enterprise in audacity that I could not help but admire. General Auchinleck was handling his forces with very considerable skill. He seemed to view the situation with decided coolness, for he was not allowing himself to be rushed into accepting a second-best solution to any moves we made."[28] General Fritz Bayerlein commented that Auchinleck's multiple counterattacks during First Alamein were tremendously successful and convinced Panzer Army Africa that all was lost. He thought it a pity that no one in Britain recognized these smaller battles Auchinleck had

---

27 Michael Carver, *El Alamein* (London: B. T. Batsford, 1963), 17-18, 26
28 Jonathan Dimbleby, *Destiny in the Desert: The Road to Alamein – The Battle that Turned the Tide of World War II* (New York: Pegasus Books, 2013), 278-300.

won during First Alamein.[29]

Rommel's defeat took Hitler completely by surprise. He realized that the losses suffered by Panzer Army Africa could not be easily replaced, and he feared this defeat was only the first step in what could become a crisis in North Africa.[30]

Sir Brian Horrocks, Montgomery's favorite general, referred to Auchinleck's heroic stand at First Alamein as the turning point in the war. "It was the desperate fighting in the fortnight of July, when the Eighth Army rescued Egypt, which paved the way for our subsequent victories."[31] Yet the eminent British military historian, J.F.C. Fuller, barely mentions the battle in his *The Second World War 1939-1945* (1993). Fuller wrote, "Orders were issued to fall back on El Alamein, where the front between the Mediterranean and the Qattara Depression narrows to thirty-six miles. El Alamein was occupied on June 30. Though for a time both sides attempted to keep the battle fluid, by the end of July the position stabilized."[32] He mentioned neither Auchinleck nor Rommel's assessment of him.

In his posthumous work, *A History of Warfare* (1983), Montgomery devoted two pages to his battles of Alam Halfa and Second Alamein. He did not even mention the Battle of First Alamein, but he did write "the Alamein position held against Rommel's assaults; it had no open flanks."[33] He devoted not a word to the significance of the battle, Auchinleck's command of it, or that it was Rommel's first defeat. These accomplishments

---

29 Correlli Barnett, *The Desert Generals* (Bloomington, N.: Indiana University Press, 1982), 225.; Liddell Hart, B. H. ed, *The Rommel Papers* (New York: Harcourt, Brace and Company, 1953), 248.
30 Walter Warlimont, *Inside Hitler's Headquarters 1939-1945* trans. R. H. Barry, (Novato, CA: Presidio, 1964), 242.
31 Brian Horrocks, *A Full Life* (London: Collins, 1960), 110-111.
32 J. F. C. Fuller, *The Second World War 1939-1945* (New York: Da Capo Press, 1993), 173.
33 Montgomery of Alamein, *A History of Warfare*, 512.

he was reserving for himself. In a most unprofessional manner, he would allocate credit to neither Auchinleck nor an Eighth Army not commanded by him.

Even Benito Mussolini was more gracious than Montgomery. In his memoirs, he wrote, "The wheel of fortune turned on July 28, 1942, when we were halted before El Alamein. We ought not to have advanced so far without the certainty of reaching Alexandria, but Rommel was pig-headed."[34]

The fighting in July, commanded by Auchinleck, was responsible for turning retreat into a counterattack. Auchinleck had taken personal command of the battle and displayed all the attributes of a great commander. His undoing, however, was his assessment that he would not be able to launch a major counterattack until mid-September. This was not acceptable to Churchill, who promptly removed Auchinleck from command. Montgomery, his replacement, was not to launch a counterattack until October 23, 1942, the Battle of Second Alamein. Its success should not be allowed to overshadow the earlier achievements of those who made it possible. Montgomery, however, would do everything in his power for the rest of his life to do just that.[35]

In early August 1942, General Alexander left England to replace Auchinleck as Commander-in-Chief Middle East, and Lieutenant General William Gott was selected to replace Auchinleck as Eighth Army Commander. Churchill remarked that he intensely disliked having to relieve Auchinleck and that it was like killing a magnificent stag. However, on August 7, Gott was killed when his aircraft was shot down. Following the advice of General Brooke, also known as Lord Alanbrooke, now Chief of the Imperial General Staff, Churchill appointed

---

34 Benito Mussolini, *Mussolini: Memoirs 1942-1943* (London: George Weidenfeld and Nicolson, 1949), 219.

35 Horrocks, A Full Life, 111.; I. S. O. Playfair, et al, *The Destruction of the Axis Forces in Africa*, vol. 4, *The Mediterranean and Middle East*, (Uckfield, UK: 2009), 119.

Montgomery Eighth Army Commander. Montgomery had neither the reputation nor stature of Auchinleck, but he was known for ruthlessness. Montgomery looked forward to the assignment; he would be commanding a real Army and serving under Alexander, with whom he thought he could work well.[36]

Montgomery would subsequently speak poorly of Auchinleck to anyone who would listen, so it was ironic that it was Auchinleck, by his own account, who first recommended Montgomery to replace him. Churchill, much to Field Marshal Alanbrooke's consternation, was determined that Gott would replace Auchinleck. He thought it would take too much precious time for Montgomery to get to Egypt from England. He even offered the command of Eighth Army to Alanbrooke, who turned it down. Alanbrooke justified his refusal on the grounds he did not know anything about desert warfare. In reality, he felt he was the only one who could maintain some control over Churchill's rashness, and he considered it his duty to continue to do so.[37]

A few weeks after the victory of First Alamein, Auchinleck would be enduring the indignity of Montgomery's unprofessional accusations that he and his Eighth Army had developed a defensive, defeatist attitude. The injustice of this slander was ludicrous. Auchinleck's lively and aggressive tactics had stopped Rommel's advance on Cairo. At the end of July, Rommel admitted in his dispatches that Auchinleck had outfought him. Auchinleck's victory over Rommel at First Alamein was in many ways more remarkable than Montgomery's victory at Alam Halfa. Auchinleck did not enjoy nearly the materiel superiority over Panzer Army Africa that Montgomery did. Nor was

---

36 Earl of Tunis Alexander, *Memoirs 1940-1945* (London: Cassel, 1962), 10.; Lord Alanbrooke, *War Diaries* 1939-1945 (Berkeley: University of California Press, 2001), 295.; John Keegan, *The Second World War,*9), 335.; Montgomery of Alamein, *Memoirs*, 70-71.
37 Dimbleby, *Destiny in the Desert*, 313-315.

Rommel's status of fuel and ammunition critically low during First Alamein, as it would be at Alam Halfa.

Churchill's decision not to retain Auchinleck and to use his abilities to their best advantage may have been his greatest mistake. The proponents of this view point out that Auchinleck would have handled the Italian campaign better, would not have taken so long to reach Caen at Normandy, and never would have made the supreme blunder of Operation Market Garden. Perhaps more importantly, Auchinleck's professionalism never would have permitted him to disrupt Allied unity by engaging in the type of subterfuge in which Montgomery excelled in order to get his way.[38]

---

38 Philip Warner, "Auchinleck," in *Churchill's Generals*, ed. John Keegan (New York: Grove Weidenfeld, 1991), 140-145.

CHAPTER III:
NORTH AFRICA

MONTY SEIZES COMMAND

General Montgomery arrived in Cairo on August 12, 1942. That morning, he met with General Auchinleck and was briefed on his plan of operations. In his memoirs, Montgomery wrote that Auchinleck said, "At all costs, the Eighth Army must be kept 'in being' and must not be destroyed in battle. If Rommel attacked in strength, as was expected soon, the Eighth Army would fall back on the Delta; if Cairo and the Delta could not be held, the army would retreat southwards up the Nile, and another possibility was a withdrawal to Palestine. Plans were being made to move the Eighth Army H.Q. back up the Nile." [39] Montgomery wrote that he listened in amazement to these plans but asked no questions. Auchinleck was to remain in command of the Eighth Army until August 15, and Montgomery used the two days before he assumed command to visit Eighth

---

[39] Viscount Montgomery of Alamein, *Memoirs*, 87.

Army headquarters.[40]

Montgomery arrived at Eighth Army headquarters on the morning of August 13. He was not impressed with what he found. Auchinleck had believed a commander should live in the same conditions as his troops when in the field. Montgomery felt the austere conditions at the headquarters were not suitable for efficient operations. He asked one of the officers where Auchinleck slept. When told Auchinleck slept on the ground next to his command truck, as tents were forbidden, Montgomery knew he would have to make changes. He met Lieutenant General W.H. Ramsden, one of the corps commanders during the visit. Ramsden was filling in for Auchinleck while he was in Cairo. Montgomery asked him about the withdrawal orders; Ramsden replied that there were orders but that they were not definite. Upon hearing this, Montgomery decided to take command of the Eighth Army on the spot. He sent Ramsden back to his corps and visited General Bernard Freyberg at XIII Corps. Later that evening, he addressed the Army staff at the headquarters. He canceled all supposed orders for any withdrawal, and told them that there would be no withdrawal, they would hold their ground, and if they could not stay there alive, they would stay there dead. Montgomery knew his actions that day had been disobedient. He later wrote, "I'm afraid that it was with an insubordinate smile that I fell asleep; I was issuing orders to an Army which someone else reckoned he commanded!"[41]

Montgomery not only was being unprofessional by seizing the reins of command before he was authorized, but he also engaged in conduct unbecoming an officer by slandering General Auchinleck with the accusation that he planned to withdraw if Rommel attacked in strength. Auchinleck's victory had set the

---

40 Ibid.
41 Ibid., 91-94.

conditions for Montgomery's subsequent success in the desert. After defeating Rommel, Auchinleck had decided to make his stand at Alamein, determined to hit back at Rommel and not expecting to retreat. But it was obviously prudent to plan for defensive positions further to the rear in case of a surprise defeat.

Montgomery went so far to write in the official "Review of the Situation in Eighth Army from 12 August to 23 October 1942" that Auchinleck's plan for the army was, if Rommel attacked, a withdrawal to the rear lines and that Auchinleck had already issued orders to that effect. Auchinleck had no intention of withdrawing from the Alamein position, and Montgomery knew it.

Montgomery's attempts to destroy Auchinleck's reputation did not end there. Until he was forced to recant by the threat of a lawsuit after his memoirs were published, Montgomery always made much of the alleged plan for the Eighth Army to withdraw to the delta if Rommel attacked again. This was a shameful attempt to cast Auchinleck's command in the gloomiest light to heighten the contrast with his own brilliant, inspired leadership. Though other commanders may have done the same, it is particularly unfortunate in Montgomery's case. His abilities and accomplishments after taking command of the Eighth Army stand on their own merit. There was no need to disparage Auchinleck.[42]

Still, Montgomery took every opportunity to emphasize the difference between the Eighth Army before he took command and after, attempting to wipe the accomplishments from the pre-Montgomery Eighth Army from the history books. The Eighth Army had been fighting in North Africa for almost

---

[42] Horrocks, *A Full Life*, 112-113.; Stephen Brooks, ed., *Montgomery and the Eighth Army: A Selection from the Diaries, Correspondence and other Papers of the Viscount Montgomery of Alamein, August 1942 to December 1943* (London: Army Records Society, 1991), 20.; Ibid., 70.

three years before his arrival, and they had prevented an Axis takeover of Egypt and had suffered 80,000 casualties. None of this meant anything to Montgomery; he was only interested in his command. Concerning the withdrawal order, General Freddie De Guingand, Montgomery's Chief of Staff, later remarked to General Horrocks "that quite unwittingly he may have overstated the importance of the withdrawal order during his first meeting with Montgomery before they arrived at Eighth Army Headquarters on August 13th."[43]

ALAM HALFA

Auchinleck knew Rommel would attack again. The defensive plan he devised for the upcoming attack of Panzer Army Africa was to hold the area between the coast and Ruweisat Ridge and to hold the Alam Halfa Ridge in strength, from which counterattacks could be launched to cut off any enemy penetrations.

Rommel knew the Axis momentum in North Africa had been halted. It was only a matter of time before the British, with American materiel aid, would permanently remove any chance for Axis victory in the desert. Rommel knew he had to attack again before British superiority in men and materiel became too great to overcome.[44]

As B.H. Liddell Hart pointed out, after the victory of First Alamein, Auchinleck began preparations for a fresh offensive by focusing British training on combined tactics. At the same time, as a precaution against another attack by Army Group Africa, he pressed on with the new defenses he envisioned. This was a defense in depth in the El Alamein area anchored on key terrain; the Ruweisat Ridge and the Alam Halfa Ridge. Hart went on to

---

[43] Horrocks, *A Full Life*, 114.
[44] J. F. C. Fuller, *The American Civil War to the End of the Second World War*, vol. 3, *Decisive Battles of the Western World and Their Influence Upon History*. (London: Cassell and Company, 2001), 482.

suggest that Montgomery was using Auchinleck's plan during the battle of Alam Halfa. "The effectiveness of Auchinleck's design was strikingly shown at the end of August when Rommel took the initiative again and made a bid for final victory. But its fulfillment was then in other hands."[45] Montgomery took Auchinleck's plan and, after analyzing it against the Ultra intelligence reports, and deciding it was a good plan, accepted it as his own. He did alter the size of the reserve as a result of the additional tanks and artillery supplied by the Americans. Giving in to his ego, he briefed General Alexander that the plan was his, making no mention of Auchinleck's contributions.[46]

Montgomery also failed to mention Major Freddie de Butts, a British intelligence officer who worked for General Horrocks. Without the benefit of Ultra intelligence, de Butts developed an assessment of Panzer Army Africa's most likely course of action for the upcoming battle that was remarkably similar to the intelligence provided by Ultra. Horrocks arranged for de Butts to brief his assessment to Montgomery before the battle. Montgomery had already studied the Ultra messages and knew what Rommel was planning to do. Rommel would launch a supporting attack in the north to fix Montgomery, and then attack with his main effort in a sweeping maneuver in the south to outflank him. Montgomery could not, of course, reveal the existence of Ultra to a mere Major, nor at that time to Horrocks. However, Montgomery would have demonstrated real professionalism by giving credit to Major de Butts for the analysis of what Rommel would do at Alam Halfa. Instead, motivated by his ego and unable to mention Ultra, he claimed all credit for himself. The combat superiority of the British and knowledge of Rommel's plan through the Ultra intercepts set

---

45 B. H. Liddell Hart, *The Tanks: the History of the Royal Tank Regiment, 1939-1945* (London: Cassell, 1959), 2:209-210.
46 Fuller, *Decisive Battles*, 483-486.

conditions for Montgomery's first victory of the war.[47]

On the night of August 30, 1942, Rommel launched his attack. Panzer Army Africa attacked with the Italian Corps and the German 90th Light Division in the north, just as Montgomery knew they would. That night, Panzer Army Africa struck in the south with the famed Afrika Korps and two Panzer divisions in the first echelon, again, just as Montgomery knew they would. Auchinleck's plan and the Ultra intercepts had told him the Ruweisat Ridge in the south would be key terrain. The ridge was heavily defended, as was Alam Halfa Ridge to the east, as called for in Auchinleck's plan. But it was here that Montgomery displayed a stroke of military genius. He left a lightly defended gap between Alam Nayil hill and the Alam Halfa Ridge, enticing the Germans to attack there so the British could attack them on the flanks. It took all night for the Afrika Korps to breach the minefields, but by morning on August 31, although harassed by the British 7th Armored Division, the famous Desert Rats, the 15th and 21st Panzer Divisions, were once again attacking. In the afternoon, the 21st headed for the gap between Alam Nayil hill and Alam Halfa Ridge while the 15th continued toward Alam Halfa Ridge. Just as Montgomery foresaw, he could launch an attack into the left flank of the 21st. By 5 p.m., the British attacking force and lack of fuel stopped the 21st, which then attempted to hold its position.[48]

During the afternoon of August 31, 1942, it became apparent to Montgomery that victory would be his. He directed his staff to plan an all-out counterattack and pursuit, and he ordered X Corps to be prepared to conduct them. This was the first indicator he had considered pursuit either before or during Alam Halfa. Yet, when Panzer Army Africa began its withdrawal, Montgomery

---

47 Horrocks, *A Full Life*, 1960), 116.
48 Ibid., 122-123.

refused to release the armored forces he had designated as the pursuit forces. He may have decided it was more prudent to wait until he had received three hundred new M4 Sherman tanks from the United States, which were due at Suez on September 3. While Montgomery was extremely competent at planning and initiating a battle, he consistently failed to follow through, first at Alam Halfa, then at Second Alamein, and then at Antwerp.[49]

Up to September 3, the battle went just as Montgomery had foreseen. The next day the 15th Panzer Division failed to make any headway against the Alam Halfa Ridge, and by evening, Rommel was forced to call off his attack. That night, the RAF's close air support had so degraded Panzer Army Africa that Rommel was forced to give up any hope of significant results from the battle.[50]

Though Rommel was no longer attacking, he was not withdrawing either. His forces remained in place throughout the day. Montgomery showed flexibility when he launched a counterattack into the enemy rear to interdict their lines of communication, a gambit known as an "indirect approach." Montgomery launched the attack on the night of September 3, using the New Zealand Division. The New Zealanders were successful, and Rommel knew he could not leave them astride his lines of communication. The New Zealand Division fought off German and Italian attacks throughout September 4. Having accomplished their mission, Montgomery withdrew them that night. Rommel decided to retreat the next day, as his forces lacked the fuel to re-engage in offensive operations and Allied

---

49 Ronald Lewin, *Montgomery as Military Commander* (London: B. T. Batsford, 1971), 60.; Montgomery, *Memoirs*, 88.
50 Montgomery of Alamein, *Memoirs*, 99.; Horrocks, *A Full Life*, 124.; Fuller, *Decisive Battles*, 488.

air support was taking a heavy toll on his men and tanks.[51]

Before going to church on the morning of September 3, Montgomery left instructions that there was to be no more than patrolling activities forward of any main battle positions. The next day, reports were coming into the Eighth Army command post that the enemy was withdrawing in three columns. That evening, General Alexander arrived to speak with Montgomery, who by this time had decided not to pursue. Alexander supported Montgomery in his decision. Rommel completed withdrawal on September 5. Everything had gone according to Montgomery's master plan, except for the need to launch a limited counterattack with the New Zealand Division.[52]

The state of Panzer Army Africa after the Battle of Alam Halfa was very advantageous for a British counterattack. Montgomery would have known this, based on Ultra and reports from his subordinate units. However, he only allowed some harassing operations by his 7th Armored Division, which were quickly beaten off. His whole conduct of the battle was very competent but cautious. There is no doubt that he passed on an opportunity of cutting off and destroying the Afrika Korps on September 1 and 2, when lack of fuel had immobilized it. If he had done so, the destruction of Panzer Army Africa would have followed.[53]

Churchill had expected Montgomery to begin an offensive by September 22. Instead, Montgomery notified General Alexander that the Eighth Army needed reinforcements, rest, and additional training. He insisted he could not launch offensive operations against Panzer Army Africa until mid-October, about a month later than Auchinleck assessed British

---

51 Montgomery of Alamein, *Memoirs*, 100.; Horrocks, *A Full Life*, 123-124.; Francis De Guingand, *Operation Victory* (London: Hodder and Stoughton, 1947), 146-149.
52 Michael Carver, *El Alamein* (London: B. T. Batsford, 1963), 71.
53 F. W. von Mellenthin, *Panzer Battles: A Study of the Employment of Armor in the Second World War* trans. H. Betzler, (Old Saybrook, CT: Konecky and Konecky, 1956), 145-146.

offensive operations could begin. Auchinleck was fired for his assessment; Montgomery was allowed to delay until October 23, 1942, in preparation for his breakout at Second Alamein.[54]

Montgomery knew his forces lacked the daring and flexibility to outmaneuver the Germans; he intended to crush them in a set-piece battle to destroy their offensive capabilities for good. This observation by John Keegan is revealing, for it indicates that perhaps Montgomery recognized his shortcomings while attempting to outfox Rommel. Also, Auchinleck had gone a long way toward destroying Panzer Army Africa's offensive power in First Alamein. The miserable failure of the German attack initiating the Battle of Alam Halfa and its unsustainability after seventy-two hours demonstrated that Rommel no longer possessed a capability to execute offensives even before Montgomery arrived in Egypt.

Montgomery needed a clear-cut victory in his first battle. This requirement, plus his caution, forced him to avoid risks. Also, he was not yet satisfied with the training and morale levels within the Eighth Army. He was not going to launch his forces into a full pursuit as long as he thought Rommel retained the capability to establish a viable defense.[55]

The intelligence Montgomery received from Ultra intercepts deserves further comment, as it relates to the battle of Alam Halfa. Royal Air Force Group Captain F.W. Winterbotham was responsible for the dissemination of Ultra intelligence from its origins at Bletchley Park in England to a select few field commanders. Montgomery was one of these commanders. The Ultra reports of August 15, 1942, supplied Montgomery the complete order of battle for Panzer Army Africa including its strength in men, tanks, artillery, and aircraft. Perhaps even

---

54 Michael Carver, *El Alamein* (London: B. T. Batsford, 1963), 85-86.
55 Keegan, *The Second World War*, 336.; Lewin, *Montgomery as Military Commander*, 61.

more importantly, it gave Montgomery Panzer Army Africa's fuel and ammunition status, which was poor. Within a few days, Ultra also revealed the plans for Rommel's upcoming attack on the British Eighth Army, the Battle of Alam Halfa.[56]

Through Ultra, Montgomery knew that Rommel would begin his assault on August 31 with a "surprise" attack through the Qattara Depression in the south on the left flank of the Eighth Army. This attack would be followed by a sweeping movement to the north, which would roll up the Eighth Army and drive them into the sea. Montgomery immediately called for a commander's conference in which he briefed Rommel's intentions as his own intuition, rather than information provided to him. Of course, Montgomery could not reveal the existence of Ultra to his subordinate commanders as only very few individuals had been cleared for Ultra messages. However, the more professional tactic would have been to credit his G2 intelligence officer or the aforementioned de Butts. Montgomery, however, knew that labeling the Ultra information as his own intuition meant that he would receive full credit for accurately assessing Rommel's intentions, credit he was unwilling to share with anyone else.[57]

In any event, Ultra had provided Rommel's plan and enough time for Montgomery to array his forces to meet Rommel's attack. Montgomery deployed his defenses in depth and anchored them on the Alam Halfa ridge, which provided excellent observation. The Afrika Korps did indeed attack across the Qattara Depression on the morning of August 31 and advanced until making contact with Montgomery's forces on the Alam Halfa ridge. The fighting was intense, but Montgomery's defense was successful. Montgomery had his first victory and was finally in the limelight. He relished it.[58]

---

56 F. W. Winterbotham, *The Ultra Secret* (NY: Harper and Row, 1974), 73.
57 Ibid., 73.
58 Ibid., 74-75.

Montgomery even kept the Ultra messages secret from his Chief of Staff. Major General Freddie de Guingand wrote in 1964 that during the Battle of Alam Halfa, Montgomery had anticipated Rommel's intentions precisely and had skillfully deployed his forces to meet the threat. De Guingand must have had a revelation about this episode in 1974 when the British government began releasing information on Ultra, and Winterbotham was able to publish a book on his wartime experiences with Ultra, *The Ultra Secret*.[59]

SECOND ALAMEIN

After his defeat at Alam Halfa, Rommel's logistical situation had so degraded that he was inclined to retreat into Libya. However, Hitler ordered him to stand fast, as the Fuhrer believed Rommel's position just west of Alamein was the most defensible in North Africa. So Rommel held his positions and prepared for Montgomery's offensive. Montgomery planned to feint toward the south to fix the German armor and then to launch his main attack in the north.[60]

On the night of October 23, 1942, Montgomery began his breakout of the Alamein position by executing Operation Lightfoot. The battle of Second Alamein had begun. This was not a surprise to the Germans. Even at the Fuhrer Headquarters, the general opinion was that Montgomery was champing at the bit and would launch an attack against Rommel, whose German and Italian forces were greatly understrength in men and tanks and were low on both ammunition and fuel. However, because Rommel held terrain that favored the defense, it was assumed he would defeat the British attack.

The battle began with engineers and infantry attempting to

---

59   De Guingand, *Generals at War*, 68.
60   Warlimont, *Inside Hitler's Headquarters*, 246.; Playfair, et al, *The Destruction of the Axis Forces*, 33-34.

breach the minefields in the north for the tanks. In the south, the British 7th Armored Division, and a Free French Brigade attacked to fix the German armor so they could not be sent north where the main attack was to take place. The next day, the British continued the slow business of breaching the northern minefields. The German commander, General Georg Stumme, died of a heart attack and was replaced by Lieutenant General Wilhelm von Thoma. Rommel was in Germany, recovering from an illness. While the main British attack waited for the minefields to be cleared, fighting broke out across the entire front. Indeed, von Thoma believed Montgomery was attacking on a broad front. Just before sunset, von Thoma launched a counterattack that was beaten off by the British 1st Armored Division.

As the sun set, Montgomery found himself badly behind schedule. Before the breakout at Alamein, Montgomery had been so concerned about a tidy battlefield and control over his forces that he had endangered the troops. He deployed them to their assembly areas the day before the main attack instead of during hours of darkness just before. Elements of the Panzer Army Africa quickly identified these assembly areas and the vulnerable Eighth Army soldiers and vehicles. The German forward observers called for artillery fire missions to smash these assembly areas, but a severe lack of ammunition kept the artillery silent. Had there been enough ammunition on hand for the Germans to fire the missions, Montgomery's attack would have been disjointed and weakened and may not have succeeded.[61]

On the morning of October 25, Rommel left Germany to return to North Africa. Also on this day, Montgomery made

---

[61] Montgomery, Viscount of Alamein. *El Alamein to the River Sangro, A Personal Account of the Eighth Army's Campaign* (London: Hutchinson, 1958), 16-19.; Alanbrooke, *War Diaries*. 50.; Ruge, *Rommel in Normandy*, 203.; Warlimont, *Inside Hitler's Headquarters*. 253.

his first change in his master plan for the battle. He added a night attack. The objective was to take Point 29. The attack was successful, and the British took over two hundred prisoners. The next morning, Rommel counterattacked, as he thought Point 29 had been Montgomery's main attack. British artillery and close air support broke up Rommel's counterattack before it could have any effect. Having been checked, Rommel decided to move some of his armored assets to the north. Montgomery, hearing of Rommel's movements, then made the second change in his master plan. He began thinning out his lines to form a reserve of the New Zealand Division and two armored divisions.[62]

On the night of October 26, the British attacked west. The primary objective was a kidney-shaped hill, a piece of key terrain called Snipe; the secondary objective was an area north of the Snipe called Woodcock. The attack toward Woodcock did not happen that night because the British got lost in the dark. Confusion was now added to the fog of war with which Montgomery had to contend. However, the attack toward the Snipe went as planned.

On the morning of October 27, the British found their way to Woodcock but ran into Rommel's forces. On Snipe, the British were fighting to defend their position, and the British at Woodcock were unable to provide any support. Sensing disaster, Montgomery dispatched a brigade to reinforce the British on Snipe. Just before sunset, and before the British reinforcements arrived, Rommel's forces overran the British on Snipe. Later that night the reinforcements reported to Montgomery that they had reached Snipe and were digging in. They did not know it, but in fact, they were lost and digging in at the wrong place, several kilometers from Snipe. Such confusion and mistakes on

---

[62] Montgomery, *El Alamein to the River Sangro*, 18-19, Playfair, et al, *The Destruction of the Axis Forces*, 43-45.

the British side were certainly not part of Montgomery's plan.[63]

On the night of October 28 to 29, the British forces that had taken Point 29 a few days earlier attacked the northwest, while Australian infantry and British tanks attacked the northeast. Montgomery was determined to keep Rommel guessing until he launched his main attack. These attacks were called off after the Australians got lost and separated from the British tanks. Montgomery showed dash and flexibility by launching these attacks, which were not part of the plan but became necessary as the battle developed. Two of them failed due to forces being lost, for which Montgomery's generalship cannot be blamed. He continued to display his flexibility by planning a new supporting attack for his main attack, which would go in on November 2, 1942. This new attack was launched on the night of October 30, from Point 29. The next day, the 21st Panzer Division counterattacked. The fighting continued through November 1 and was inconclusive both sides sustained heavy casualties but also lost large amounts of fuel. This was a decisive factor in Rommel's future planning. The fuel situation in Panzer Army Africa was now critical, and Rommel knew the battle could not be won.[64]

By October 29, the battle had turned into one of attrition. It had lasted for five days, the British had achieved little, and an impatient Churchill was beginning to regret appointing Montgomery.[65] The impression in London was that Montgomery was allowing matters to end without any decisive result; Churchill complained to Alanbrooke that Montgomery had done nothing for three days. Alanbrooke immediately went to the defense of Montgomery. Churchill responded, "Why had he

---

63 Playfair, et al, *The Destruction of the Axis Forces*, 53-57.; Montgomery, *El Alamein to the River Sangro*, 20.
64 Ibid., 53-57.
65 Carver, *El Alamein*, 157-159.

told us he would be through in seven days if all he intended to do was to fight a halfhearted battle?"[66] Alanbrooke was able to calm the Prime Minister down by explaining how Montgomery had inflicted enormous losses on Panzer Army Africa over the last week. One is entitled to wonder if Alanbrooke defended Auchinleck against Churchill's ranting with the same passion with which he defended Montgomery.

In the meantime, Montgomery was doing exactly what he would later claim he never did, changing the plan. By this time, Rommel was down to 116 German tanks and 220 Italian tanks. Though he had failed to break out, Montgomery was winning the battle of attrition.

In the early morning hours of November 2, 1942, Montgomery began his main attack, Operation Supercharge. The objective was the enemy base at Tel el Aqqaqir. In another display of flexibility, Montgomery had changed its focus from the north to the south. The attack began with seven hours of artillery and aerial bombardment. The New Zealand Division led the land charge with ninety-four British tanks. Many of the German and Italian anti-tank guns were still in position, and Montgomery knew there were great risks involved. After a few hours of hard fighting, the New Zealanders and British had secured their objective. The cost had been high—two-thirds of the British tanks had been knocked out—but the battle of Second Alamein had been won. At 11 a.m. Rommel counterattacked and was successful in destroying almost one hundred British tanks, but the counterattack failed.[67]

That night, Rommel decided to withdraw west to Fuka. He sent a message to Hitler informing him of his decision. On November 3, Hitler replied that Rommel was to, once again,

---

66 Alanbrooke, *War Diaries*, 335-336.
67 Montgomery, *El Alamein to the River Sangro*, 22.; Playfair, et al, *The Destruction of the Axis Forces*, 67-70.

stand fast. Rommel decided to leave the German 90th Light Division and two Italian Corps, which had no transportation assets, to dig in as a rear guard while the rest of Panzer Army Africa prepared to withdraw west.

Montgomery attacked the same night again. The rear guard held but was slowly being wiped out. Rommel once again asked Hitler for permission to withdraw. No reply was forthcoming from the Fuhrer, and after consulting with his Theater Commander, Field Marshal von Kesselring, Rommel decided to execute the withdrawal. Benito Mussolini wrote that the British, by use of massed artillery effects and American tanks in their armored formations "broke through and turned the Italian infantry positions, which led to one of the greatest retreats in history. Most of the Italian infantry became prisoners because of a lack of motor transport and were marched to those infamous and notorious prison cages."[68]

In the darkness of the early morning hours of November 4, 1942, Panzer Army Africa began its withdrawal. In his initial attempts at pursuit, on November 5, Montgomery sent the 7th Armored Division down the coastal road and the 1st Armored Division through the desert to cut Rommel off. The 7th moved too slowly, and the 1st ran out of fuel. The next day, the remnants of Panzer Army Africa beat off an attack by the 7th.[69]

News of Rommel's defeat at Second Alamein did not cause much anxiety at the Fuhrer Headquarters, but the successful Allied landings in West Africa did. These landings, Operation Torch, took place on November 8, 1942, Hitler blamed the success of Operation Torch on the Luftwaffe, as they were the only German asset in a position to interdict the landings and had failed to do so. On November 19, news came in that

---

68   Mussolini, *Mussolini: Memoirs*. 4.
69   Montgomery, *Memoirs*, 93.

the Soviets had broken through the Romanians southwest of Stalingrad. The campaign in North Africa was thus not a priority for the German high command. Mussolini felt that Rommel, after the defeats at First Alamein and Alam Halfa, should have withdrawn to Mersa Matruh before Montgomery initiated the Battle of Second Alamein. Had Rommel done so, he would have had a month to strengthen the defenses at Mersa Matruh.[70]

During the battle, Montgomery had displayed the qualities of a great commander. Indeed, the level of competence he showed before the withdrawal of Panzer Army Africa had outshone even Rommel. However, once Rommel began to withdraw, a new Montgomery seemed to emerge. As Omar Bradley recounted, "Having knocked Rommel senseless, Montgomery failed to deliver the coup de grace. He let the remnants of Panzer Army Africa slip away."[71]

Montgomery's caution dismayed official London. Rommel wrote "The British had assembled powerful armored forces between Alam Halfa and Bab el Qattara and had then remained stationary in their assembly areas. Local attacks followed, but they were easily beaten off. The impression we gained of the new commander, General Montgomery, was that of a very cautious man, who was not prepared to take any sort of risk."[72]

In a debriefing interview after the war, German General Fritz Bayerlein disclosed that he was amazed at the ease with which Rommel was allowed to escape after Second Alamein, stating "I do not think General Patton would have let us get away so easily."[73]

On November 10, Montgomery wrote the Chief of the Imperial General Staff, General Alanbrooke, that the failure to cut off

---

70 Engle, *At the Heart of the Reich*, 139-141.; Mussolini, *Mussolini: Memoirs*, 219.
71 Omar Bradley, *A General's Life* (New York: Simon and Schuster, 1983), 122
72 Liddell Hart, ed., *The Rommel Papers*, 248.
73 Michael Arnold, *Hollow Heroes* (Oxford: Casemate, 2015), 63.

and destroy Rommel was due to the rain that bogged down his pursuing units. The rain, however, did not seem to have the same effect on Rommel's units. If Montgomery had initiated pursuit twenty-four hours earlier, just after Rommel had withdrawn, the New Zealanders could have established a blocking position, preventing any further retreat of the remnants of Panzer Army Africa. Montgomery then could have destroyed Rommel's remaining forces in detail. He had a crushing superiority in every category of combat power, and he knew it through Ultra reports. Much has been written about the rain that slowed the Eighth Army pursuit of Panzer Army Africa, so much so that one would think it rained only on the British. The same rain that slowed the British pursuit also slowed Rommel's retreat, especially since a good part of Panzer Army Africa was on foot, and because of a lack of fuel, many of Rommel's vehicles had to be towed, slowing them even more. Panzer Army Africa could have and should have been destroyed in November 1942 instead of May 1943, but it was not to be. The whole concept of pursuit is, once the enemy has begun a withdrawal, to maintain contact with him, keep him on the run, and deny him any opportunity to regroup, defend, or counterattack. The objective is always to fix and destroy the enemy. Just as Napoleon emphasized, time is the most crucial element in combat operations. If the enemy is allowed time to establish a course of action against the pursuing force, he will.[74]

Before the Battle of Second Alamein, Alexander was in constant conference with Montgomery, Tedder, and Coningham. All four argued it out very carefully. Above all, Alexander told Montgomery, "You need to beat this army, not put it to flight."[75] This was in accordance with his initial orders to destroy Rommel and his Army. According to Nigel Hamilton, Montgomery's

---

74 Keegan, *The Second World War*, 337
75 Alexander Clifford, *Three Against Rommel: The Campaigns of Wavell, Auchinleck and Alexander* (London: George G. Harrap and Company, 1943), 305.

official biographer and close friend, Montgomery bungled his chance of destroying Panzer Army Africa after Second Alamein through a display of confusion, lack of communication, and incoherent command. Indeed, Montgomery knew more about the locations and dispositions of Rommel's units than he did his own. Montgomery refused to acknowledge this, and in his later writings and memoirs left out any mention of the confusion that reigned in Eighth Army on November 4 to 5. To change the whole concept of the Eighth Army's operations from an armored *coup de grace* at Alamein to one of pursuit across North Africa is in itself an acknowledgment that Montgomery's plan failed.[76]

Instead of acknowledging that he had to change his tactics several times during the battle, Montgomery persisted in his efforts to describe his most famous victory as one that had gone entirely according to plan. To preserve the illusion that all of his strategies went exactly the way he expected, he wrote in his memoirs that he changed his plan for Alamein two full weeks before the battle began. Initially, he planned to destroy Rommel and deal with the unarmored portion of his army at leisure. However, on October 6, he claims he changed his mind and decided just to contain Rommel's armor and to go after his infantry through a crumbling process. While it is true that this new plan went forward, it is blatantly false that it was determined upon on October 6, before the battle. To his credit, at Second Alamein, Montgomery made this alteration to his plan in the middle of the battle on October 26, after his armor failed to break out of the minefields. This was when the infantry crumbling process began.

In short, the Battle of Second Alamein was not the military masterpiece that Montgomery always claimed it was afterward. Multiple episodes of confusion at key points and times on the

---

76   Hamilton, *Master of the Battlefield*, 26-29.

battlefield resulted in changes to Montgomery's initial plan. Montgomery's refusal to admit this was unfortunate because the changes he made displayed decisiveness and flexibility, neither of which characterized his generalship after the victory of Second Alamein.[77]

The contribution of Ultra to Montgomery's success at Second Alamein was just as significant as it was at the Battle of Alam Halfa. The Germans were unaware Ultra was exploiting their communications. Immediately after his capture at Second Alamein, General Wilhelm Ritter von Thoma was invited to dine with Montgomery. According to Thoma, Montgomery said that "instead of asking me for information, he would tell me the state of our forces, their supplies, and their dispositions. I was staggered at the exactness of his knowledge, particularly of our deficiencies and shipping losses. He seemed to know as much about our position as I did myself."[78] Of course, Montgomery would claim all the credit for this knowledge for himself.

Second Alamein had been a resounding success for Montgomery. There had been other British victories over the Afrika Korps and Panzer Army Africa in the desert, but Second Alamein was the first time the enemy, and especially Rommel, had been put to flight. Churchill ordered church bells rung throughout England. Montgomery became a national hero overnight, and he reveled in the limelight. There was also a certain poignancy about Second Alamein for the British people, for if one discounts the three hundred American Sherman Tanks and one hundred self-propelled artillery pieces supplied in time for the battle, it was to be the last victory the British would achieve without the significant assistance of the United States.

All of this affected Montgomery's generalship, and it showed

---

77 Montgomery, *Memoirs*, 109.
78 Liddell Hart, *The German Generals*, 164-165.

during the initial pursuit of Panzer Army Africa. In addition to the celebrity he had won, he attained the reputation as the Allies' greatest general. This was a reputation he would spend the rest of the war, and his life, trying to maintain. In doing so, he would also earn another reputation, that of an overcautious general who would fight only when victory was assured. As a result, the Allied war effort would suffer.[79] Montgomery, as a well-read student of war, should have heeded the words of von Clausewitz: "The importance of the victory is chiefly determined by the vigor with which the immediate pursuit is carried out. Pursuit makes up the second act of the victory, and in many cases, is more important than the first."[80]

THE PURSUIT

During Second Alamein, Montgomery's Chief of Staff De Guingand held several planning sessions to develop a self-contained pursuit force available for when the need arose. De Guingand finished the plan, but it was never implemented because of the confusion among the Eighth Army forces when the time came for the pursuit. Montgomery's first real attempt at pursuit began on November 5, 1943, with the British X Corps, consisting of three armored divisions and the New Zealand Division, advancing west across the desert to cut Rommel off at Fuka. The objective of the 1st Armored Division was El Daba. 10th Armored Division was to take Ghazal. The New Zealand and the 7th Armored Divisions headed for Fuka. The 1st and 10th Armored Divisions made contact with the remnants of Italian XXI Corps, part of Rommel's rear guard, and completed their destruction.

Rommel was able to escape because the New Zealand and 7th Armored Divisions were halted south of Fuka by a dummy

---

[79] Trevor Royle, *Montgomery: Lessons in Leadership from the Soldier's General* (New York: Palgrave Macmillan, 2010), 74.
[80] Carl von Clausewitz, *On War* (Princeton: Princeton University Press, 1976), 267

minefield. Even though Panzer Army Africa was critically short of fuel, they were able to continue their withdrawal. By November 10, Panzer Army Africa had passed Mersa Matruh, Side Barrani, and Bardia, leaving them for the British. Though Montgomery was on the heels of Rommel, he decided to halt and wait to be resupplied. The best opportunity for Montgomery to fix and destroy Rommel was over.[81]

As mentioned above, Montgomery blamed the failure to destroy Rommel on the rain, writing, "Heavy rains interfered with my plans. The force was bogged down and its fuel and supplies were held up some miles behind."[82] The Eighth Army Chief of Staff, General De Guingand also felt this was the case, writing, "I doubt whether many people realize how near Montgomery was to destroying the retreating remnants of Rommel's forces, and that only a most unlucky break in the weather deprived him of his prize."[83] Rommel's forces, to be sure, were more critically short of supply and fuel than Montgomery's, and the rain that fell on Montgomery also fell on Rommel. Commanders of the highest order overcome obstacles such as weather and logistics to complete their tasks. In the aftermath of Second Alamein, Rommel proved to be such a commander. Montgomery did not. Montgomery was not going to suffer a setback against Rommel, no matter how insignificant, after his victory at Second Alamein.

After the failure of the initial pursuit, Montgomery spent November 10 tidying up the battlefield, Rommel continued his westward movement, and twenty-four vital hours were lost. At this point, Panzer Army Africa consisted of five thousand soldiers, twenty tanks, twenty anti-tank guns, and about fifty pieces of artillery. Rommel had enough fuel to withdraw but not

---

81 De Guingand, *Operation Victory*, 210.; Playfair, et al, *The Destruction of the Axis Forces*, 86-87.
82 Montgomery, *El Alamein to the River Sangro*, 25.
83 De Guingand, *Operation Victory*, 212.

to fight. The sea guarded his northern flank, but his southern flank was wide open. This is why Montgomery's decision to halt for twenty-four hours was so unfortunate. Panzer Army Africa was ripe for the picking. Rommel knew he had to get to a defensible position, and Montgomery's halt would allow him to do that. Rommel was heading to El Agheila, also known as the Mersa Brega line. Though Montgomery failed to prevent Rommel from reaching El Agheila, he was able to occupy Tobruk on November 13, 1943, and Benghazi on November 20. Rommel had destroyed the port facilities in Benghazi before abandoning the city.[84]

Soon after the British occupied Benghazi, two announcements were made. First, Montgomery was promoted to full General. Second, his staff announced they had a plan to cut Rommel off before he reached El Agheila. The plan called for sending a force to cut off Panzer Army Africa south of Benghazi while they were moving toward El Agheila. De Guingand thought it was an excellent plan, but Montgomery would not hear of it. He refused to risk the possibility that Rommel would counterattack and defeat this force. De Guingand and the staff knew that at that time, Rommel did not have the resources to launch any attack. A solid opportunity to destroy Panzer Army Africa was missed because Montgomery was more concerned with protecting his reputation.[85]

Rommel arrived at Agedabia on the Mersa el Brega line on November 19. Panzer Army Africa had virtually no fuel left and was now too far from Italy to receive fuel by air; the nearest fuel depot was 250 miles to the west. The terrain at El Agheila favored the defense; it was surrounded by soft ground

---

[84] Bruce Watson, *Exit Rommel: The Tunisian Campaign, 1942–43* (Mechanicsburg, PA: Stackpole, 2006), 27.; *Playfair*, et.al., *The Destruction of the Axis Forces*, 101-103. Liddell Hart, ed., *The Rommel Papers*, 354.
[85] De Guingand, *Operation Victory*, 216.

and broken irregular land where armored vehicles could not maneuver. Even so, Rommel wanted to bypass El Agheila and withdraw into Tunisia. He knew he could only hold El Agheila if he received adequate logistical and air support. He also knew these commodities would not be forthcoming, because the Axis forces in Tunisia now fighting the British First Army, which included the American II Corps, was the priority for support. However, Rommel received an order from Mussolini directing him to hold the Mersa el Brega Line; this order was followed by a message from Hitler confirming Mussolini's order. On November 28, Rommel flew to Berlin to confer with Hitler. Hitler reiterated the stand-fast order, and a disappointed Rommel departed for Africa. However, Mussolini had been having second thoughts, and on November 30, got Hitler to agree to a withdrawal. Rommel decided to start withdrawing his forces on December 6.[86]

On November 29, Montgomery completed his plan for defeating Rommel at the Mersa el Brega line. The XXX Corps, commanded by Lieutenant General Oliver Leese, was to attack early morning on December 17. The 51st Highland Division and the 7th Armored Division were to conduct frontal attacks on Rommel's positions while the New Zealand Division was to execute a two-hundred-mile flanking march on Rommel's right to deny Panzer Army Africa the capability to withdraw. The New Zealanders would begin movement four days before the main attack because of the distance they had to travel. Even though Panzer Army Africa could not defend the Mersa el Brega, Montgomery would not risk an immediate attack. He needed time to organize his logistics. The time Montgomery spent tidying up the battlefield, Rommel used to plan and execute his withdrawal.[87]

---

86 Liddell Hart, ed., *The Rommel Papers*, 355-356.; Ibid., 359.; Playfair, et al, *The Destruction of the Axis Forces*, 219.
87 Playfair, et al, *The Destruction of the Axis Forces*, 221.

Rommel was concerned. He believed Montgomery would not attack until mid-December; however, if the British discovered his withdrawal, he was sure Montgomery would strike at once. On December 9, patrols from XXX Corps reported that elements of Panzer Army Africa were withdrawing. Instead of attacking immediately, Montgomery changed the attack date to the early morning of December 15, giving Rommel six more days. Rommel detected British reconnaissance patrols active on his right, and with the sea guarding his left flank, he correctly assessed what Montgomery's attack plan was.[88]

In accordance with that plan, the New Zealand Division began its movement early on December 11. To support the New Zealand Division, Montgomery started an artillery bombardment and a ground attack against some of Rommel's strong points to distract Rommel, hoping the New Zealanders would be able to bypass unnoticed. Rommel, already sure the British would attempt to outflank his left, did detect the New Zealanders, though he could not determine which British unit they were. He wanted to attack them with his two panzer divisions, but he did not have the fuel for a fight. Because of the artillery attacks and the attacks on his strong points, Rommel believed Montgomery was launching his main attack and immediately began withdrawing the rest of his forces. He had already withdrawn the non-motorized Italian and German elements of his Army. The Panzer Army Africa lost twenty tanks, and five hundred Germans and Italians were taken prisoner. Montgomery called these losses significant; this indicates he knew very well how depleted Rommel's forces were, as the loss of twenty tanks in a clash of two armies would be minor. Rommel believed Montgomery made a huge mistake; Montgomery should have known the poor state of Panzer Army

---

[88] Liddell Hart, ed., *The Rommel Papers*, 370.; Playfair, et al, *The Destruction of the Axis Forces*, 224.

Africa's combat capabilities, and that Panzer Army Africa would not accept battle at Mersa el Brega. Therefore, he should not have attacked Rommel's strong points until after the New Zealanders had passed Rommel's right flank. When Montgomery did launch his main attack on December 14, Rommel's forces had withdrawn, and XXX Corps fought only the rear guard. Another opportunity for destroying Panzer Army Africa was lost. The Montgomery of Alam Halfa and Second Alamein, who had made timely decisions to change his course of actions, had become the overcautious Montgomery that refused to take an opportunity if there was risk involved.[89]

By December 18, 1942, Rommel had withdrawn to Buerat. At this point, Montgomery was not Rommel's primary concern. He was worried the British First Army, fighting in Tunisia, would seize the Gabes Gap and eliminate any possibility of a junction between Panzer Army Africa and the Fifth Panzer Army in Tunisia. Rommel, who by now had ample opportunity to learn Montgomery's habits, knew Montgomery would take the time to tidy up the battlefield before attacking the Buerat position.[90] Just before he withdrew from Mersa el Brega, Rommel wrote, "Montgomery has shown himself to be overcautious, he risks nothing, and bold ventures are foreign to him. I am quite satisfied that Montgomery will never take the risk of following up boldly and overrunning Panzer Army Africa, which he could do without any danger to himself."[91] Montgomery knew he would have to face Rommel at Buerat, but first, he had to halt to build up stocks of supplies. Indeed, Montgomery wrote, "The tempo of my operations was determined by administrative considerations."[92]

---

[89] Montgomery, *El Alamein to the River Sangro*, 30-31.; Liddell Hart, ed., *The Rommel Papers*, 371-372.
[90] Liddell Hart, ed., *The Rommel Papers*, 360,
[91] Ibid., 376-377
[92] Montgomery, *El Alamein to the River Sangro*, 30-31

Rommel had established a blocking position with the 15th Panzer Division at Sirte to delay any attack on Buerat. By mid-January 1943, Montgomery felt ready to attack the Buerat position. By this time he had attained a four-to-one advantage in infantry and almost an eight-to-one advantage in tanks. Montgomery intended to prevent the enemy from withdrawing in order to destroy him, and once the attack began, his forces were to go right to Tripoli without any delay imposed by the enemy. To set conditions for the battle, he attacked the 15th Panzer Division at Sirte on December 24; the Germans immediately withdrew to Buerat. However, on December 25, Montgomery paused for reinforcements.

On January 1, 1943, Rommel received permission to withdraw from Buerat and move to the Tarhuna-Homs Line. He was also directed to delay the British before Tripoli for six weeks. Also, he was directed to detach the 21st Panzer Division to the Fifth Panzer Army, reducing his combat power even further.[93]

Montgomery attacked January 15. Panzer Army Africa held throughout the day and, to escape encirclement, withdrew that night. Rommel intended to fight a delaying action. For the first time during the pursuit, Montgomery directed that operations were to continue day and night. On January 19, the British entered Homs. Realizing the possibility of being encircled, Rommel ordered the 90th Light Division and the remnants of the old Afrika Korps to delay the Eighth Army. Everyone else was ordered to Tripoli. Rommel also ordered the destruction of the port facilities there. On the night of January 23, Rommel withdrew from Tripoli, and the next morning, Montgomery entered the city.[94]

---

[93] Montgomery, *Memoirs*, 137-138.; Liddell Hart, ed., *The Rommel Papers*, 380-382,; Ibid., 384.

[94] Liddell Hart, ed., *The Rommel Papers*, 385.; Playfair, et al, *The Destruction of the Axis Forces*, 234-236.

After taking Tripoli, Montgomery decided to pause to build up his logistical advantage. This allowed Panzer Army Africa, now only a division's worth of combat power, to carry away some supplies it had stored outside the city. Rommel decided next to occupy the Mareth Line, an old French series of small fortifications. The Italians were angry with Rommel for abandoning the Tarhuna-Homs Line and Tripoli. They tried to convince Hitler to recall Rommel. In the meantime, the last chapter in the pursuit was about to be written.[95]

The Eighth Army spent the month of February pushing the remnants of Panzer Army Africa, now called the German-Italian Panzer Army, out of Libya and into the Mareth Line. Montgomery's pressure on Rommel was so weak that Rommel was able to receive the 10th Panzer Division, plan and execute an offensive in support of the Fifth Panzer Army, and inflict a significant defeat on the U.S. II Corps to prevent capture of the Gabes Gap. Realizing the Americans needed help, General Harold Alexander, the 15th Army Group Commander, ordered Montgomery to step up the effort against the German-Italian Panzer Army to relieve some pressure on the Americans. This Montgomery did, and by February 26, Rommel had to break off his offensive against the Americans.[96]

Montgomery believed, now that Rommel had the 10th Panzer Division, that Rommel would launch an attack against the Eighth Army. He was correct. However, on March 3, Rommel gave up command of the German-Italian Panzer Army to General Messe. Rommel was promoted to Commander, Army Group Africa, which consisted of the Fifth Panzer Army and the German-Italian Panzer Army. On March 6, 1943, Messe attacked the Eighth Army at Medenine with three divisions. The

---

95 Liddell Hart, ed., *The Rommel Papers*, 390.
96 Playfair, et al, *The Destruction of the Axis Forces*, 291-297.; Montgomery, *Memoirs*, 142.

attack was unsuccessful; Montgomery had too much combat power. As the German-Italian Panzer Army withdrew back to the Mareth Line, Montgomery refused to pursue and went back to planning his set-piece attack on the Mareth Line. On March 9, Rommel departed Africa for consultations with Hitler; he would never return. General Hans-Jurgen von Arnim took command of Army Group Africa.[97]

The Mareth line was anchored on its left by the sea and on its right by rugged hilly terrain. That terrain could be bypassed, though it would be a difficult proposition. The importance of the Mareth Line was that it was the key to the Gabes Gap. Montgomery's plan was the same as he had repeatedly used against Rommel, a frontal attack and a left hook to outflank the enemy and destroy him. X Corps would conduct the frontal attack, and the New Zealand Division with the French Brigade would provide the flanking force. On March 14, the French and New Zealanders began movement to their assembly area in the mountains on the enemy right and closed on the assembly area on March 18, the move was not detected, Montgomery had learned a lesson at Mersa el Brega, and there were no attacks on the Mareth Line during this move. The next day, the flanking force continued their advance around the Mareth Line.

On March 17, the American II Corps captured Gafsa and continued toward El Guettar. The result was the 10th Panzer Division, the most combat capable unit in the German-Italian Panzer Army, was directed to pull out of the Mareth Line. This weakened the Mareth Line considerably. On March 20, the enemy identified the flank attack of the French and the New Zealanders, but there was little they could do but monitor it. Therefore, Montgomery launched the first stage of his frontal attack by committing the 50th Division down the coastal road.

---

[97] Montgomery, *Memoirs*, 143.

An enemy counterattack stopped the division, but it was able to hold its positions until Montgomery withdrew it on March 23; however, the Germans and Italians were beginning to react to the flank attack.[98]

Montgomery decided to reinforce the flanking force with the X Corps held in reserve. In the early morning of March 26, the French and New Zealanders punched a hole in the right flank of the German-Italian Panzer Army, and the 1st Armored Division immediately passed through. For the first time in the pursuit, Montgomery had successfully executed an indirect attack. During the night of March 27, the remnants of the German-Italian Panzer Army withdrew from the Mareth Line, leaving behind 7,000 prisoners.[99]

SUMMARY

Doctrinally, the pursuit ended when Tripoli fell to the Eighth Army, the Battle of the Mareth Line was its result. This battle showed Montgomery could learn from mistakes. He did not open his preparatory fires or launch elements of his main attack too soon, as he had done at Mersa el Brega. During the Battle of the Mareth Line, Montgomery also somewhat changed his impression of the Americans. He had consistently called the Americans amateurs at war, but he saw how they could fight when Patton's U.S. II Corps attacked Gabes to relieve pressure on the Eighth Army. On March 23 the battle was joined, and the II Corps, led by the 1st Infantry Division also known as the "Big Red One," defeated the 10th Panzer division and forced it to withdraw. Patton had come to Montgomery's aid, and the Americans had defeated the Germans on the battlefield for the first time in the war.

---

98 De Guingand, *Operation Victory*, 239.; Ibid., 247-248.; Playfair, et al, *The Destruction of the Axis Forces*, 348.
99 Playfair, et al, *The Destruction of the Axis Forces*, 350-351.; De Guingand, *Operation Victory*, 262-263.

Montgomery's erstwhile opposite, Field Marshal Rommel, possessed some of Montgomery's negative traits as well. It seems Rommel's insubordinate ambition hampered his relations with peers and superiors. Few people dared oppose him on an issue because of the way he brutally exploited his patronage by people in high places, including Hitler.[100]

From the time Montgomery assumed command of the British Eighth Army in North Africa in August 1942, he enjoyed an overwhelming superiority of resources over the enemy. This simple fact, rather than any military prowess, may be the basis for his successes. Indeed, the essence of Montgomery's method was that one should not commit oneself against the enemy until one has assembled the forces of all arms and the logistical resources to succeed. Except for one disastrous exception, Market Garden, Montgomery could not be dissuaded from his military art. This has led some to claim that with Montgomery's material superiority in North Africa, any competent General could have defeated Rommel's forces and done so faster.[101]

Montgomery's desire to protect his reputation by avoiding even minor risks made him predictable and assisted the retreat of Panzer Army Africa. The Eighth Army offensive operations in Egypt gave Field Marshal Kesselring an idea of Montgomery's strategy. Kesselring thought Montgomery would always choose a safe course of action; therefore, he tended to be methodical in his operations. Rommel consequently knew Montgomery would always allow him the time to break contact, withdraw quickly, and maintain an orderly and efficient retreat.[102] Rommel wrote,

---

100 Rick Atkinson, *An Army at Dawn* (New York: Henry Holt, 2002), 439-443.; Clifford, *Three Against Rommel*, 381; Franz Halder, *The Halder War Diary 1939-1942*. Eds., Charles Burdick and Hans-Adolf Jacobson (Novato, CA: Presidio, 1988), 454.
101 Michael Carver, "Montgomery," in *Churchill's Generals*, ed. John Keegan (New York: Grove Weidenfeld, 1991), 149.
102 Kesselring, *Memoirs*, 140.

"Nowhere was Montgomery able to destroy us. The speed of his reaction was comparatively low. In the earlier stages of the retreat, his outflanking columns were too weak, and we could have attacked and destroyed them on several occasions, but we did not have the petrol. Montgomery should have put his main weight behind these outflanking drives as these had the greater chance of bringing us to battle."[103]

Montgomery's concern for his reputation even made it to the desk of Field Marshal Alanbrooke, the Chief of the Imperial General Staff. In his entry for December 15, 1942, Alanbrooke wrote that he investigated the many rumors and accusations that Montgomery was far too sticky, thought only of his reputation, would never take risks, and played for certainties. Alanbrooke, of course, felt these accusations were unjustified. However, after the war, when officers felt free to write of their war experiences and assess Montgomery's generalship, it became apparent that the number of high-ranking officers critical of Montgomery was legion and not just American.

Montgomery's refusal to put the destruction of Panzer Army Africa above preserving his reputation was the most unprofessional aspect of his service in North Africa. There was, however, another.[104]

Auchinleck was not the only senior officer in North Africa whose reputation Montgomery tried to diminish. He also attacked Lieutenant General Kenneth Anderson, his counterpart commanding the British First Army. These attacks began in February 1943, when Montgomery wrote to Brigadier F.E.W. Simpson that Anderson should not be the commander to take Tunis. He was doubtful that Anderson was "the chap to handle the show."[105]

---

103   Liddell Hart, ed., *The Rommel Papers*, 395.
104   Alanbrooke, *War Diaries*, 349.
105   Brooks, ed, *Montgomery and the Eighth Army*, 131.

Also that month, he wrote the Chief of the Imperial Staff, Field Marshal Alanbrooke. Montgomery told Alanbrooke that he had heard from a friend on Anderson's staff that Anderson did not know how to run an Army headquarters. He also wrote he would mention it to General Alexander, the 15th Army Group Commander and Anderson's boss. Montgomery was relentless, again writing Alanbrooke on March 17, "From what I have heard from other sources, it would seem that Anderson is quite unfit to command an Army in the field."[106]

Montgomery was slandering a fellow Army commander to the Chief of the Imperial Staff based on rumor, not on personal observation or experience. What he wrote was not only unprofessional, it was unethical. Not content with this, he wrote Alanbrooke again on April 12 that "Anderson is no good and not up to it; remove him at once and put in a proper chap."[107] Now Montgomery apparently felt he could tell the Chief of the Imperial Staff how to do his job.

In his memoirs, Montgomery took one last swipe at Anderson, claiming that it was he, not Anderson, that developed the final plan for the capture of Tunis.[108] When published in 1958, the claim caused quite a stir. Field Marshal Alexander felt compelled to defend Anderson, writing in his own memoirs published in 1962, that Montgomery had nothing to do with the attack on Tunis. General Omar Bradley was less blunt, writing "Montgomery claimed full credit for the final plan that led to the capture of Tunis and for the final victory in Tunisia, and he was able to get the British press to give him the credit. Ike was furious, he held a press conference to clear up the misconception, but the truth never really caught up with Montgomery's lie."[109]

---

106 Ibid., 136.
107 Ibid., 207.
108 Montgomery, *Memoirs*, 148-149.; Alexander, *Memoirs*, 38.
109 Bradley, *A General's Life*, 159.

The last bit of unprofessionalism concerns the awarding of the Eighth Army Bar to the Africa Star Campaign Medal to those who fought in North Africa. Only those British soldiers assigned to the Eighth Army after October 23, 1942 were authorized to wear it. The War Ministry pettily forbade it to those who were killed or wounded severely enough to be evacuated from Africa before then. The ministry continues to this day not to explain this injustice. As that date coincides with the start of the battle of Second Alamein, it is difficult not to see Montgomery's hand in the sordid affair.[110] General De Guingand wrote that he was always puzzled over the issue and remarked that Montgomery was cruel and unjust in pursuing it.[111]

---

110 Nigel Nicolson, *Alex* (London: Weidenfeld and Nicolson, 1973), 157-164.
111 Francis De Guingand, *From Brass Hat to Bowler Hat* (London: Hamish Hamilton, 1979), 5.

CHAPTER IV:
SICILY

PLANNING

Undoubtedly, the most important strategic decision in the war made by the Anglo-American alliance was the "Germany first" strategy; however, the Americans and British had different concepts of how to accomplish this. The Americans felt the most efficient way to support the Russians and threaten Germany was to invade Europe through France. The British believed in the soft-underbelly approach to Europe, through the Mediterranean. They were convinced it would take a year or more to assemble the men and resources for a cross-channel invasion. The British view was the one adopted by the Allies, and so the next logical step was an invasion of Sicily, the stepping stone to Italy, christened Operation Husky. The Combined Chiefs of Staff again selected General Dwight D. Eisenhower as Supreme Allied Commander for Husky, as he had been for Operation Torch. General Harold Alexander, as the 15th Army

Group commander, was Eisenhower's subordinate commander of the Allied land forces.[112]

Alexander recalled that there were four good ports in Sicily: Messina, Catania, Syracuse, and Palermo. Both Syracuse and Palermo were within fighter coverage range and not heavily defended. The original invasion plan designated the two cities as D-Day objectives. The soundest administrative plan was to land the U.S. Seventh Army, commanded by Lieutenant General George Patton at Palermo, and the British Eighth Army, still under the command of Montgomery at Syracuse.

After examining the plan, Montgomery concluded it was unsound. An American landing in the northwest in the vicinity of Palermo would leave Montgomery's forces, landing in the southeast between the Gulf of Catania and Gela, unprotected on their left flank. Montgomery did not concur with this dispersion. On May 2, 1943, Montgomery attended the conference in Algiers, where he immediately made his views known. He convinced Eisenhower to shift the assault of the Seventh U.S. Army from the northwest and Palermo to the southeast in the vicinity of Gela to protect the Eighth Army's left.[113]

Montgomery had, of course, devised his own plan for the taking of Sicily. It included concentrated assault landings in the southeast, with the Eighth Army landing south of Syracuse and the Seventh Army landing around Gela. He also called for two more divisions to be added to the Eighth Army to allow him to capture airfields quickly en route to Catania. The initial plan was more to the liking of the American commanders and the British naval and air leadership. Even so, on May 13, 1942, only two months before Operation Husky was to begin, Eisenhower

---

112   Wasserstein, *Barbarism and Civilization*, 327.; Montgomery, *El Alamein to the River Sangro*, 69.
113   Alanbrooke, *War Diaries*, 417.; Montgomery, *El Alamein to the River Sangro*, 70-72.

approved Montgomery's plan.[114]

Not only did changing the plan anger other senior officers, especially the Americans, but Montgomery's unwillingness even to consider the opinions of his superior officers and peers degraded Allied cohesion. His showmanship and arrogance irritated even Eisenhower. Under strict instructions from General George C. Marshall to develop an Allied team, Eisenhower had relieved several American officers who had been critical of their British counterparts. As Supreme Allied Commander, he also had authority to relieve British officers who were critical of Americans, but he always refrained from doing so.[115] If he had held all officers to the same standard, many British officers would have been relieved as well. Montgomery certainly would have.

Alanbrooke had to, in his words, "haul Monty over the coals for the trouble he was creating through his usual lack of tact and egotistical outlook which prevented him from considering other people's point of views."[116] He also felt Montgomery's attitude toward a bet he had made with Bedell Smith in North Africa for a flying fortress had laid the foundation for Eisenhower's dislike and, more importantly, distrust of Montgomery. Smith, Eisenhower's Chief of Staff, thought the bet was a joke; however, Montgomery demanded payment and Eisenhower had to deliver the aircraft to Montgomery for his personal use.[117]

The change in the Seventh Army's landing area from Palermo to Gela meant the airfields around Palermo would remain in enemy hands. The situation greatly angered Air Marshal Tedder. Also, failing to secure the Port of Palermo meant having to resupply the Seventh Army over the beach in the vicinity of Gela. The resulting concentration of shipping upset Admiral

---

114 Baldwin, *Battles Lost and Won*, 195.; Montgomery, *Memoirs*, 157.
115 Baldwin, *Battles Lost and Won*, 201-202
116 Alanbrooke, *War Diaries*, 418.
117 Montgomery, *Memoirs*, 201-202

Cunningham, the operation's senior British Naval officer. However, Montgomery would have his airfields and his Port at Syracuse for resupply, and his left would be protected while he took Messina. That is what mattered to him.[118]

There were no complaints from Patton about the change in the plan. When approached by Alexander, who attempted to console him, Patton commented that he only followed orders, he did not plan. Alexander, like Patton, knew that landing the Americans in the south instead of at Palermo would increase the difficulty of the Seventh Army mission significantly. Unlike Montgomery, Patton would not have the use of a port until he took Palermo. Patton even commented to Admiral Cunningham that he did not care what beach he landed on, he would still get to Messina.[119]

Alexander later wrote that the attitude of the Americans "was an example of the complete loyalty and inter-Allied cooperation which inspired all operations with which I was associated in the Mediterranean theater."[120]

Montgomery's plan entailed that the Eighth Army, the main effort, would land on Sicily between Syracuse and Pozallo, seize Catania, then capture Messina and cut the German escape route to Italy, forcing the Germans to surrender. For this task, he had four infantry divisions, a separate infantry brigade, an airborne division, and three armored brigades. The plan relegated General Patton's Seventh Army, landing at Gela, to the supporting effort; Patton would protect Montgomery's left. The Seventh Army consisted of four infantry divisions, one airborne division, one armored division, two separate armored battalions, and three

---

[118] Nicolson, *Alex*, 195
[119] Samuel Morison, *Sicily – Salerno – Anzio January 1943 – June 1944*, vol. 9, *History of United States Naval Operations in World War II* (Chicago: University of Illinois Press, 2002), 20.
[120] Alexander of Tunis, *Memoirs*, 106-108.

tank destroyer battalions.[121]

Montgomery was still not content. On May 2, without giving Patton the professional courtesy of a consultation, he wrote Alexander demanding that Patton detach one of his corps to the Eighth Army. Also, Montgomery wrote he ought to be placed in overall command of all ground operations, including Patton's Seventh Army. Indeed, he wished to have the entire Sicily campaign transformed into an Eighth Army show.

Though Alexander was patient with Montgomery, he disapproved the proposal. Had he accepted it, there would have been two repercussions. First, placing Montgomery in command of all ground operations would be a delegation of Alexander's role and responsibilities as the commander of 15th Army Group. This, Alexander was too professional to allow. Second, Alexander knew the Americans were still angry about his decision to designate the Eighth Army as the main effort and would not agree to transfer one of Patton's corps to Montgomery. The Americans would likely reply that if Montgomery did not possess enough combat power to accomplish his mission, the Eighth Army should have been placed in the supporting role with the Seventh Army as the main effort.[122]

On June 2, 1943, Montgomery briefed his plan for Operation Husky to Churchill and the Combined Chiefs of Staff in Algiers. General George Marshall, the U.S. Army Chief of Staff, was not impressed with Montgomery, and he agreed with Field Marshall Alanbrooke that Montgomery needed a lot of educating to make him see the whole picture of the operation and not just what was in his Eighth Army orbit. Marshall conceded that Montgomery was a hero in Britain and a great trainer of men, but his lack of

---

121 John Strawson, *The Italian Campaign* (London: Martin Secker and Warbug, 1987), 109.
122 D' Este, *Bitter Victory: The Battle for Sicily*, 1943 (New York: Harper Perennial, 2008), 124.; Montgomery, *Memoirs*, 163-164.

tact and disdain for others' points of view were likely to lead him to commit many errors.[123]

CATANIA

According to Allied intelligence, the disposition of the enemy was becoming clearer. The island garrison consisted of two German armored divisions and five Italian infantry divisions. The Italian contingent also contained six coastal divisions dispersed around the island. The enemy's disposition showed that they considered the southeast the most probable location for an Allied landing. This is where both the Seventh and Eighth Armies were now headed.[124]

On the night of July 9, 1943, the Allies landed in Sicily. The British faced little opposition, but the Americans had to beat off several attacks. The most severe fighting took place in the Seventh Army center. At Gela, the Americans repulsed two Italian attacks. The 16th U.S. Infantry Regiment of the 1st Infantry Division repulsed two Italian tank companies with the help of naval gunfire. A few hours later, the regiment fought off ninety tanks from the Herman Goering Division. The next day, a German regiment supported by seventeen Tiger tanks overran a battalion of the 140th Regiment of the 45th Division. By the end of July 10, Patton's forces had secured their beachheads and taken 4,000 prisoners. Both the American and British lodgment areas were successfully established.[125]

On July 12, Montgomery began his move to Catania. He directed XIII Corps to advance along the coast. Lieutenant General Oliver Leese's XXX Corps was to advance to Leonforte, southwest of Mount Etna and in the Seventh Army Zone. By July 13, Kesselring had to admit that the Italian coastal defense

---

123 Montgomery, *Memoirs*, 164.; Pogue, *George C. Marshall*, 218.
124 Montgomery, *El Alamein to the River Sangro*, 75.
125 Morison, *United States Naval Operations*, 113-117.; Ibid., 145.

had failed and that the Italian troops were of limited utility. Therefore, he reported to Hitler that the German forces on hand could not hold the island. Hitler responded by himself taking direct command over German operations on Sicily. July 13 was a day of slow progress, and Montgomery came to realize there was a high potential for the Eighth Army and Seventh Army to overlap. Commanders take great pains to ensure this type of situation does not occur on the battlefield. When a friendly unit (the Eighth Army) crosses the boundary of another (the Seventh Army), it creates confusion and a real potential for fratricide. This boundary change put Highway 124 in the British zone. In effect, Montgomery, without any coordination, was maneuvering the XXX British Corps directly in front of Lieutenant General Omar Bradley's II U.S. Corps. Realizing the danger he had caused, Montgomery asked Alexander to change the Eighth Army's boundary with the Seventh Army. Alexander concurred. All Montgomery had to say about it after the war was that the 15th Army Group put things right by making Highway 124 inclusive to the Eighth Army.[126] Bradley later wrote, "What followed was the most arrogant, egotistical, and dangerous move in the whole of combined operations in World War Two."[127] This boundary change was the most controversial incident in the campaign, and it severely disrupted the Seventh Army's operations.

Bradley was incensed. The 45th Division was just one kilometer from Highway 124. Now Bradley would have to pull that division thirty kilometers back to the beach, pass it through the rear of the 1st Division, and then move it to the left of that division. This was dangerous, as it could disrupt II Corps logistical operations. Bradley could have moved the 45th Division in a day if he had been allowed to use Highway 124, but Montgomery had already

---

126 Warlimont, *Inside Hitler's Headquarters*.), 335-336. Montgomery, *El Alamein to the River Sangro*, 80.
127 Bradley, *A General's Life*, 188.

taken possession of it. Now the Seventh Army was forced to halt and make way for Montgomery's forces. In addition to angering the Americans, Montgomery's actions disjointed the U.S. II Corps. The Seventh Army was ready to break out, they were well organized, logistics were running smoothly, and the enemy was withdrawing from their front and concentrating at Catania before Montgomery. Patton's Army was set and ready to execute a fast assault on the northern coast, then turn toward Messina before the enemy could establish a cohesive defense of the city. If not for this British tactical blunder, the U.S. II Corps could have cut off the 15th Panzergrenadier Division from its escape route toward Messina.[128]

General Leese came to believe Montgomery's change of plan was a mistake. He felt the American's were much better than Montgomery gave them credit for, and if Montgomery had not encroached upon the road, the Americans would have driven straight up it and the campaign would have ended much sooner. Montgomery could not admit he was in error, and when his "left hook" failed to advance, the whole logic of his strategy fell apart. Montgomery's controversial maneuver relegated the mission of the Seventh Army to merely guarding the Eighth Army's left.[129]

Patton was furious that his army was being assigned a defensive role while Montgomery was allowed to attack. Patton believed he could attack northwest, take Palermo, cut the Island in half, and get to Messina before Montgomery could. However, Patton was being held back so Montgomery could make the main effort further east. Patton would write, "Alex has no idea of either the power or speed of American armies. We can go twice as fast as the British and hit harder, but to save British prestige, the XXX Corps had to make the

---

128   Omar Bradley, *A Soldier's Story* (New York: Henry Holt, 1951), 136 - 138.; Royle, *Montgomery: Lessons in Leadership*, 96.; Bradley, *A General's Life*, 188.
129   Hamilton, *Master of the Battlefield*, 308.

envelopment."[130] However, Montgomery's progress was so slow that, to his chagrin, Alexander would have to take the leash off Patton. On July 15, the 15th Army Group directed the Seventh Army to develop operations to the north, which would permit them to cut the northern coastal road. With the Eighth Army's left secured, Montgomery thought he could thrust to Leonforte and Adrano to get around Mount Etna. This would allow him to get behind the enemy at Catania. On July 17, Patton went to see Alexander to propose the use of his and Montgomery's armies in the advance on Messina. The proposal was well timed, as on July 18, Montgomery's attack on Catania, supported by both an amphibious and airborne operation, failed.[131]

Knowing he was in a quagmire before Catania, Montgomery decided to shift his focus to Leese's XXX Corps. Alexander now also realized Montgomery had taken on a task at Catania that he could not complete. On July 20, Alexander directed that Patton was to turn east and attack alongside Montgomery toward Messina, Montgomery on the right and Patton on the left. By July 21, it was clear to Montgomery that the Germans were going to continue to hold the Catania plain. On July 22, the Seventh Army's "Provisional Corps," commanded by Major General Geoffrey Keyes, took Palermo, and the next day, Bradley's II Corps cut the northern coastal road. With great disappointment, a few days before his ouster, Mussolini had to acknowledge that his Italians in the western and central Sicily were beaten and were heading to Allied prison camps, while the Germans had fought with great valor everywhere, especially in the Catania plain. Now Patton could turn east to Messina. In fairness to the British, it must be acknowledged that most of the enemy forces Patton fought before his eastward pivot to Messina were Italians

---

130 Martin Blumenson, ed., *The Patton Papers 1940-1945* (Boston: Houghton Mifflin, 1974), 204.
131 Bradley, *A Soldier's Story*, 144-145.

and Sicilians not willing to die for Mussolini. The British faced the bulk of the German forces throughout the campaign.[132]

To get around Mount Etna, General Leese's XXX Corps attacked Enna on July 28, but they failed to take the city. There was a significant enemy presence there. Therefore, without coordinating with Bradley, Leese decided to withdraw and bypass Enna to the South. Montgomery's subordinates were now using his methods. This maneuver left Bradley in a dangerous situation; Leese had created an open flank, and Bradley's right was unprotected. Bradley sent a message to Leese informing him of the danger his uncoordinated action had caused to II Corps. Then Bradley told Leese his 1st Division would cross Leese's XXX boundary and take Enna to remove the threat. Leese agreed and apologized for the trouble he had caused.[133]

On August 1, Montgomery sent XXX Corps to attack toward Adrano, as he felt that was the key to the Etna position. Montgomery's assessment was correct. Adrano fell on August 6, and the Germans began pulling out of the Catania plain for fear of being encircled. The Eighth Army could now continue its advance toward Messina. However, as the Americans had been discovering for a week, taking Messina would not be an easy task. Patton wrote, "These mountains are the worst I have ever seen. It is a miracle that our men get through them, but we must keep up the steady pressure."[134]

MESSINA

The terrain in northeastern Sicily was mountainous and would not support mass armored maneuver; it favored the

---

132 David Fraser, *And We Shall Shock Them: The British Army in the Second World War* (London: Book Club Associates, 1983), 263-266.; Mussolini, *Mussolini: Memoirs*. 45-46.; Bradley, *A Soldier's Story*, 146.
133 Bradley, *A Soldier's Story*, 143.
134 Montgomery, *El Alamein to the River Sangro*, 80.; Blumenson, ed., *The Patton Papers*, 309.

defense. The remaining Italian and German soldiers were using it to their advantage in establishing delaying positions. In this part of Sicily, there would be no armored dashes into the enemy rear by Patton or overwhelming massed attacks by Montgomery. The slowness of Montgomery's attacks south of Catania and around Mount Etna, as well as Patton's operations in western Sicily, allowed the Germans to bring in additional forces. Specifically, the arrival of the 29th Panzergrenadier Regiment helped delay the capture of Messina, resulting in possibly the most successful mass evacuation of military forces in history.[135]

It was during the drive to Messina that Montgomery and Patton worked together for the first and only time during the war. They held two previous meetings to coordinate their operations. Montgomery hosted the first at Syracuse on July 25; Patton hosted the second at Palermo on July 28. Patton and Montgomery worked well together during this final phase of the Sicily campaign.

Historians have written much of the "race to Messina." Montgomery seems never to have mentioned a race. Patton only referred his desire to beat Montgomery to Messina to those around him and in his diaries. General De Guingand did, however; make a public statement about a "race" in his memoirs, *Operation Victory* (1946), between the Seventh and Eighth Armies. The campaign in Sicily is the only campaign where a comparison can be made between Montgomery and Patton, as they were both army commanders: in Africa, Patton commanded a corps and Montgomery an army; in France, Patton commanded an army and Montgomery an army group.

Montgomery thought Patton was an aggressive saber-rattler ignorant of air-ground integration and the principles of logistics. Patton felt Montgomery was overcautious and did not trust him.

---

[135] Montgomery, *El Alamein to the River Sangro*, 86-90.; Kesselring, *Memoirs*, 165.

They were not friends. But they were brothers in the profession of arms and had a grudging respect for each other. Ironically, during the European campaign, Patton was the only American general who thought Montgomery's "single thrust into the heart of Germany" concept was valid. The only change to it Patton would have made was to make himself, not Montgomery, the leader of that single thrust. Both generals had their good and bad military aspects, but in the final drive to Messina, terrain and enemy delaying actions condemned both Patton and Montgomery to a plodding advance.[136]

On August 13, 1943, the Seventh Army took Randazzo. This was the key to the German defenses, and the next day the enemy began to withdraw all along the Eighth Army front. During this time, Patton launched several amphibious operations, unofficially referred to as "end runs," to outflank the successive German positions along the coastal road. The Germans were able to identify these "end runs" through aerial reconnaissance and make appropriate changes in their defensive dispositions. The Germans could thus delay Patton, but not stop him. The end was inevitable. The U.S. 3rd Division would be the first to enter Messina.

On the night of August 16, 1943, Major General Lucian Truscott sent a message to Patton, notifying him that the 3rd Division had entered Messina at 10:00 p.m. Taking a lesson from Patton, Montgomery launched an amphibious operation that same night, landing a commando group and some tanks at Ali in front of XXX Corps. However, the enemy had already withdrawn. This commando unit joined the Americans in Messina the next day. The campaign for Sicily was over.[137]

---

[136] De Guingand, *Operation Victory*, 301.; Blumenson, ed., *The Patton Papers*, 301.; Carlo D'Este, *Patton: A Genius for War* (New York: Harper Collins, 1995), 598.

[137] Montgomery, *El Alamein to the River Sangro*, 91.; Warlimont, *Inside Hitler's Headquarters*, 355.; Blumenson, ed., *The Patton Papers*, 309.

SUMMARY

The fall of Messina marked the end of the Sicilian campaign, which cost the Germans 24,000 lives. Montgomery, in *El Alamein to the River Sangro* (1958), chose not to mention the fact that was evident to all, the large number of Germans and Italians that got away. Eisenhower had initially thought the operation would take two weeks, but those fourteen days stretched into thirty-eight. The superb German delaying actions deserve some credit for this, but Montgomery's invasion plan, his cautiousness, and the inter-Allied squabbling, much of which he initiated, deserve blame. The invasion plan, as executed, was his, and no one except him was happy with it. That plan positioned Allied forces on the island that set the conditions for successful enemy delaying action. Montgomery's strategic conception was both disadvantageous to the American Seventh Army and disparaging to it as a fighting force.[138]

How did a small, outnumbered, and outgunned German force, without either naval gunfire or air support, prevent Montgomery's Eighth Army from breaking through and continuing to Messina? The answer lies in Montgomery's generalship during the assault on the Germans in the vicinity of Catania, in which used only a portion of the combat assets available to him. In his original plan, Montgomery intended to do an amphibious end run to outflank Catania. This would have regained the initiative and given him control of the coastal road to Messina. For some reason, though, he canceled the amphibious operation. He also made poor use of the available air assets. During the entire battle for Catania, he failed to request even one sortie of close air support. Perhaps he was not up to

---

138 Montgomery, *El Alamein to the River Sangro*, 91.; Hanson Baldwin, *Battles Lost and Won*, 197.; Albert Garland and Howard Smyth, *Sicily and the Surrender of Italy* (Washington D.C.: Office of the Chief of Military History United States Army, 1965), 420.

such a fluid combat situation.[139] Air Marshal Tedder claimed, "Montgomery was a fellow of average ability who has gotten such a buildup that he thinks himself as Napoleon; he is not."[140]

Montgomery changed the initial plan to suit his Eighth Army. He was not responsible for the successful execution of Operation Husky, so he was not bothered by the effects his plan would have on other participants in the operation. He arranged for his army a concentrated base in southeastern Sicily, pulled Patton's army in close when he felt he needed protection on his left, and then pushed them away when he wanted room to maneuver. Montgomery's selfishness harmed Anglo-American relations for the rest of the war. This was the crux of Montgomery's unprofessionalism, motivated by egomania. He was only concerned with setting the conditions for his command's success and cared not a bit about other commanders' successes or failures.[141]

The Germans compared the success of their evacuation of Sicily with Dunkirk; however, the only real similarity between the two was a morale boost for the Germans, just as morale had increased in British forces in 1940. There, the similarities end. The German evacuation was well planned, deliberate, and flawlessly executed. The Germans and some Italians escaped to Italy, fully equipped and ready to fight, as they would demonstrate at Salerno, Monte Cassino, and Anzio. Had the Seventh Army followed the original plan and landed at Palermo, Patton would have been in position on July 10 or 11 to drive for Messina. One is entitled to wonder how many Germans and Italians would not have escaped if Messina had been captured seven to ten days before it was.[142]

---

139 D' Este, *Bitter Victory*, 396-397.
140 Bradley, *A General's Life*, 166.
141 Nicolson, *Alex*, 195.
142 D' Este, *Bitter Victor*, 548.

Although Operation Husky had failed in its primary objective to destroy the Axis forces there, it did secure Allied lines of communication through the Mediterranean to the Middle East. However, since the war in North Africa had concluded, this was a hollow achievement. As far as supporting the Russians, Husky did not lead the Axis to divert one division from the east. Every one of the five German divisions sent to reinforce Italy came from France.[143]

---

143 Keegan, *The Second World War*, 349.

CHAPTER V:
ITALY

On August 17, 15th Army Group decided that Italy would be invaded by the British Eighth Army across the straits of Messina (Operation Baytown), and the Fifth U.S. Army at Salerno (Operation Avalanche). The X Corps was detached from the Eighth and allocated to the Fifth. Montgomery was left only with the XIII Corps, commanded by Lieutenant General Miles Dempsey, and V Corps, commanded by Major General Charles Allfrey. Operation Baytown was scheduled for September 3 and Operation Avalanche for September 9. The Fifth, commanded by Lieutenant General Mark Clark, was comprised of the VI U.S. Corps, under Major General Ernest Dawley, and the X British Corps, commanded by Lieutenant General Richard McCreery.[144]

Montgomery's Eighth found itself in the supporting role for the invasion. It was to draw off German forces from the Salerno area to facilitate the landings by the Fifth, the main effort.

---
144 Montgomery, *El Alamein to the River Sangro*, 99.

Montgomery did not believe Operation Baytown would achieve the desired results; he thought the Germans in his designated area of operations would refuse battle and withdraw north. For these reasons, he opposed the whole concept and complained to Alexander. Alexander responded with further orders. "Your task is to secure a bridgehead in the toe of Italy . . . If the enemy withdraws from the toe, you will follow him up with such force as you can make available, bearing in mind that the greater the extent to which you can engage enemy forces in the southern tip of Italy, the more assistance you will be giving to Avalanche."[145]

On September 3, 1943, Montgomery's Eighth Army landed at Reggio, Italy opposite Messina. There was little opposition, but from there, the advance up the toe of Italy was agonizingly slow. There were attempts to speed up progress through landings at Pizzo and Bagnara. Even though these were successful operations, they failed to increase the pace of the Eighth Army. The terrain was difficult and very restrictive. The Germans took advantage of this, and Montgomery's advance was barred and delayed by demolitions on both road and rail lines. Montgomery was becoming frustrated with his secondary role, much as Patton had been in Sicily. He began to blame Alexander, claiming that the 15th Army Group commander had no plan for Italy.

On September 5, Alexander flew to Reggio to meet with Montgomery. There, he told him the Italians had signed an armistice. Montgomery did not think that would make much difference to the Italian campaign. He also heard that Avalanche would proceed on September 9, and he would be receiving his V Corps that day as well. The V Corps would land at Taranto.[146]

At 3:15 am on September 9, Fifth Army began landing operations at Salerno. While not all D-Day objectives were

---

145 Montgomery, *Memoirs*. 171-173.
146 Fraser, *And We Shall Shock Them*, 269.; Montgomery, *El Alamein to the River Sangro*, 103.; Montgomery, *Memoirs*, 174-175.

secured, the Fifth had taken enough key terrain to establish a beachhead. On September 10, the Germans reacted in force, massing against Clark's beachhead, and almost drove his Fifth Army back into the sea. German units were arriving from Naples, and elements of the 16th Panzer Division were already engaged with Clark's forces. Clark was not yet worried because he knew that the Eighth Army was advancing north to support the Fifth. What Clark did not know was the slowness with which Montgomery was moving.[147]

Montgomery claimed his slow movement toward Salerno was the result of fighting three hundred miles and advancing in just seventeen days against an enemy that could easily delay them through their expert use of demolitions. However, only a rear guard from the 76th Panzer Corps was opposing Montgomery. Its use of natural and artificial obstacles was expert, but they only slowed Montgomery's already slow and very cautious pursuit. The Eighth was not posing a serious threat to the German forces in the vicinity of Salerno.

Also, since the British Public Records Office released the official War Diaries under the thirty-year rule in the 1970s, additional information has become available, calling Montgomery's story about demolitions into question. Montgomery's Royal Engineers stated that while there were a good number of bridges destroyed, the riverbeds were flat and dry and damaged sections of the roads were easy to bypass. There was also a team of five journalists, led by Christopher Buckley, who departed Nicastro, behind British lines, on Tuesday, September 14, to travel to the Salerno Beachhead. Later that day, they ran into another team of journalists. None had seen any Germans. The following day, they encountered yet another team of journalists, this one led by

---

[147] Mark Clark, *Calculated Risk* (New York: Enigma Books, 2007), 156-161, Martin Blumenson, *The Battle of the Generals* (New York: William Morrow, 1993), 63.

Evelyn Montague of the Manchester *Guardian,* and the Eighth Army Public Relations Officer. Again, no Germans had been seen. At 10:50 am the next morning, they ran into American engineers from the Fifth Army, who were about to destroy a bridge. Upon greeting the journalists, they realized the road to the Eighth Army was open and removed the charges. Whatever had slowed Montgomery down, it was not the Germans.[148]

Not until September 14 was there any important advance northwards. The achingly slow pace of Montgomery's Eighth Army advance toward Salerno angered Clark and concerned Alexander. Alexander had sent several messages to Montgomery ordering him to increase his haste.[149] However, they did not seem to have any effect on Montgomery, who had told Patton at Sicily, "If you get an order you don't like, just ignore it. That is what I do."[150] In reply to the first message, Montgomery told Alexander it was impossible for him to move major forces forward until he received additional resources.[151]

On September 15 a courier arrived from Montgomery, with a message for Clark stating that the Fifth Army may be having "not too good a time" and that the Eighth Army was on the way. Clark replied that the situation at Salerno was well in hand. On September 17, Clark got guidance from the Army Group Public Affairs Officer on what he was allowed to say to correspondents. "First, play up the Eighth Army's progress henceforth. Second, the Fifth Army is pushing the enemy back on its right flank. Americans may be mentioned. There should be no suggestion the enemy has made good his escape." After what the soldiers had been through at Salerno, it was difficult to understand

---

148 Richard Lamb, *Montgomery in Europe* 1943-1945 (New York: Franklin Watts, 1984), 43-44.; Kesselring, *Memoirs,* 186.
149 Fraser, *And We Shall Shock Them,* 269.
150 Blumenson, *The Battle of the Generals,* 64.
151 Montgomery, *El Alamein to the River Sangro,* 105.

the reasons for the orders to play down the Fifth Army's achievements and to play up the operations of the Eighth Army.[152]

While the Eighth Army may have posed a threat to the Germans, it did not affect the battle of Salerno. By the time Montgomery arrived in strength, that fight had already been decided. Montgomery did not play Blucher to Clark's Wellington, though like Waterloo, Salerno was a near-run thing. Regardless of the Public Affairs guidance, by early morning on September 16, the threat to the beachhead was eliminated. The Fifth Army's courageous fighting, with their backs to the sea, beat back both the 16th Panzer and Herman Goering Panzer Divisions.[153]

General Clark remarked on the influence of the Eighth Army on the battle at Salerno, "From the BBC we were told that the Eighth Army was coming to our rescue. I remember sending Monty a message that we needed help. The faster he could get, and the nearer he could get, the very momentum of his Army coming up was a deterrent to the enemy and a boost to us. But there was not any physical joining of the hands to the extent that the British came to intervene in the battle. Monty sent me some sort of personal message saying that we had joined hands, and I said, well, I have not felt the grip of your hand yet."[154]

In his mind, Montgomery believed he had saved the Fifth Army at Salerno. After the war, he wrote, "During the period of September 13 to 15, the situation at Salerno remained serious, and we continued to try to improve our maintenance situation to speed up our advance toward Salerno. Though enemy resistance to Eighth Army was not strong, the restrictive terrain and demolitions increased our demand for resources. In an effort to speed up our advance I sent patrols from my 5th Division forward to make contact with Fifth Army on September 15. The next day

---

152 Clark, *Calculated Risk*, 171-172.
153 Fraser, *And We Shall Shock Them*, 269.
154 Nicolson, *Alex*, 218

these patrols made contact with patrols from the Fifth Army. I think Eighth Army made better time than the Germans thought possible. The enemy around Salerno began to disengage in the face of the growing threat from Eighth Army."[155]

After the breakout of the beachhead and as the Fifth Army was advancing on Naples, Montgomery arrived to see Clark for the first time since Sicily. Clark asked Montgomery to join him in taking Naples. Montgomery replied that the Eighth Army was greatly extended, and they could provide no assistance to the Fifth Army as they drove on Naples. Montgomery's arrogance dismayed Clark to the point that he decided to take Naples on his own and to do the same with Rome. He needed no help from Montgomery.[156]

After the successful landings at Salerno, the Fifth Army was assigned the Mediterranean half of Italy and the Eighth the Adriatic side. For the next four months, Montgomery moved slowly up "his" side of Italy. Clark moved no faster on "his." As winter approached, the weather began to make operations even more difficult. As it had been in northeast Sicily, the terrain was of significant advantage to the enemy. On Christmas Eve, 1943, Montgomery was ordered back to England to assume command of the 21st Army Group from General Bernard Paget, and he departed Italy on December 31. During Montgomery's four months with the Eighth Army in Italy, his forces had advanced 480 kilometers, against very little opposition, to the River Sangro, a rate of about 4 kilometers per day; in Sicily, it had taken the Eighth Army forty days to advance 180 kilometers, almost the same rate of movement.[157]

Montgomery may have felt relief when leaving Italy to take

---

[155] Hamilton, *Master of the Battlefield*, 421.; Montgomery, *El Alamein to the River Sangro*, 107-108.
[156] Clark, *Calculated Risk*, 173.; Blumenson, *The Battle of the Generals*, 64.
[157] Montgomery, *Memoirs*, 182-183.; Arnold, *Hollow Heroes*, 134.

over a new command for Operation Overlord. The official British history of the Italian Campaign remarked that Montgomery had the unusual gift of combining bold speech and very cautious action. It went on to state, "A methodical orthodoxy now defined his generalship. Again and again, he chose limited objectives which he attacked only after a painstaking accretion of men and resources in such quantities that he could scarcely fail, and then the cycle would begin on the next limited objective."[158] Montgomery knew his methods would not carry the day north of the River Sangro.

Nor were they of much significance south of it. Montgomery's formula for success in Italy was the same as in North Africa. First, build up such superiority in all arms as to make defeat virtually impossible, amass enormous amounts of munitions and supplies, and then conduct preliminary air and artillery bombardment of the enemy into oblivion, followed by an overwhelming methodical ground attack. This process worked in North Africa, but in Sicily and especially in Italy, where the Germans were delaying, the time required for such a process played directly into German hands and even contributed to German success. Montgomery never learned that what worked at Alam Halfa or Second Alamein might not work against an enemy with a different intent. Montgomery ground the Eighth Army to a halt after crossing the Sangro River. Fortunately for him, Churchill pulled him out of his stalemate in Italy before he ruined his reputation.[159]

Before he left Italy, Montgomery took the time to write Lord Louis Mountbatten, Supreme Allied Commander, South East Asia Command. He told Mountbatten, who was not in Montgomery's chain of command, that the 15th Army Group

---

158 Rick Atkinson, *The Day of Battle: The War in Sicily and Italy 1943-1944* (New York: Henry Holt, 2007), 300-301.
159 Fuller, *The Second World War*, 270.; Lamb, Montgomery in Europe, 58.

commander, General Harold Alexander, had no "grip" on the 15th Army Group: there was no policy, no planning, just indecision and hesitation, and that in his estimation, Alexander's ineffective command led to a great waste of time and was an administrative scandal. This disloyalty to his commander and friend was blatantly unprofessional, and this conduct would carry over into his next campaign.[160]

---

160 Strawson, *The Italian Campaign*, 34-35.

CHAPTER VI:
NORMANDY

PLANNING

In May 1943, as a result of the Washington Conference, it was decided that there would be a cross-channel invasion of France. The code name adopted for the operation was "Overlord." A team was assembled to begin planning Overlord. It was called Chief of Staff to Supreme Allied Commander, or "COSSAC," and led by an Englishman, Lieutenant General F.E. Morgan. The Combined Chiefs of Staff at the Quebec Conference in August 1943 produced, reviewed, and approved a tentative plan. After the Teheran Conference in November 1943, it was announced that General Eisenhower would be the Supreme Allied Commander for the cross-channel invasion. Montgomery saw COSSAC's plan for the first time on December 31, 1943, at Marrakesh while returning to England from Italy. His initial response was that the landing forces were too weak, and the beachhead not wide enough.[161]

Montgomery read the plan in detail that night and very early the next morning gave his feedback to Churchill. Montgomery thought it was impracticable. He reiterated the landing front was not wide enough. A beachhead should only support one corps; a good port must be secured at the earliest possible time. Montgomery's main complaint was the seaborne assault of only one corps with three divisions against the Atlantic Wall was not adequate. Montgomery believed a sufficient force would consist of two armies, one British, the other American, each to consist of two to three corps. Montgomery would later add a landing beach on the Cotentin Peninsula, which would facilitate the capture of Cherbourg.[162]

Eisenhower agreed with Montgomery's assessment and delegated to him the responsibility for modifying the COSSAC plan. This included planning the operations to be executed after the breakout. Montgomery had always questioned Eisenhower's competence, and now he saw this delegation to him as confirmation of that impression. Only Montgomery and no one else could perform this critically important task, and he began his work with supreme confidence. Once again, Montgomery would do away with an initial plan and devise his own. However, unlike the changes he made in the plans for Dieppe and Sicily, his Overlord plan would result in a decisive victory in Normandy.

While Montgomery was responsible for the initial operational level of war on the continent, Eisenhower remained responsible for the strategic level. His strategic directive was issued to him by the Combined Chiefs of Staff, and it was simple and clear: "You will enter the continent of Europe and, in conjunction with the other Allied Nations, undertake operations aimed at

---

[161] Viscount Montgomery of Alamein, *Normandy to the Baltic* (London: Hutchinson and Company, 1946), 3-4.; Montgomery, *Memoirs*, 189.

[162] Montgomery, *Normandy to the Baltic*, 7.; Montgomery, *Memoirs*, 191-192

the heart of Germany and the destruction of her Armed Forces."[163] The relationship between Montgomery and Eisenhower would change on September 1, 1944, when Eisenhower took command of all ground operations, thus becoming responsible for the strategic and operational execution of the war in Europe.[164]

Montgomery insisted upon another major change: the use of airborne forces to secure both flanks of the landing area in Normandy. The 2nd British Airborne Division accomplished this mission on Montgomery's left and the 82nd and 101st Airborne Divisions on his right. These airborne operations were crucial to the success of the D-Day landings, as they prevented any serious enemy interference in the most vulnerable areas of the Allied attack. Montgomery was clearly incorporating his lessons learned from the ill-fated raid on Dieppe (by attacking to secure the flanks) and from Second Alamein (by using only one corps on each beachhead to minimize confusion). Montgomery made the changes and briefed Eisenhower on January 21, 1944. The Supreme Allied Commander approved Montgomery's plan.[165]

On May 15, Montgomery briefed his approved plan to all senior officers involved in Operation Overlord, Churchill, and the King also attended. In his memoirs, Montgomery devotes a total of four lines to what some call the most important mission briefing in history. These sentences precede a half-page of text devoted to his lunch that day with Field Marshal Jan Smuts. Montgomery may not have wanted to remind readers that this briefing raised the most controversial issue of the execution of Operation Overlord: the date for the capture of Caen.[166]

Montgomery allowed no note-taking, as it was a classified briefing but Omar Bradley remembered that Montgomery

---

163 Montgomery, *Memoirs*, 198.; Blumenson, *The Battle of the Generals*, 74.
164 Dwight Eisenhower, *Crusade in Europe* (New York: Doubleday Books, 1948), 225.
165 Carlo D'Este, *Decision In Normandy* (New York: E. P. Dutton, 1994), 65.
166 Montgomery, *Memoirs*, 212.

declared "British forces would take Caen on D-Day, and then over the next month advance ten miles eastward to secure the hub on which the American forces would pivot. He then placed his pointer south of Caen, almost to Falaise, and said he hoped to knock about down here with his tanks on D-Day."[167] The COSSAC planners had identified Caen as a key objective. Montgomery recognized its importance as well. The subject of Caen and the six weeks required to capture it have at times overshadowed Montgomery's great victory at Normandy.

The Germans were willing to fight desperately to hold on to Caen, as it was a critical transportation hub. Therefore, Montgomery's presence in the vicinity of Caen attracted the bulk of the best German combat formations. This included most of the German armored divisions in France. Allied air superiority delayed these German units and reduced them by losses, but they retained considerable combat capability when they arrived at Caen.

Montgomery's response was to claim that Caen had never been a D-Day objective, that drawing the German armored divisions toward Caen to facilitate an American breakout had always been his plan. If he had been more honest, if he had acknowledged the delay in taking Caen was due to massive enemy reinforcement and that he changed his tactics to attracting the German armor to facilitate the American breakout, he would have been lauded for his flexibility.

One of the German units sent to Caen was the 2nd SS Panzer Division (Das Reich). This unit had committed one of the worst atrocities in the European theater of war, at Oradour-sur-Glane. At 2:15 p.m. on June 10, 1944, elements of the 2nd SS Panzer Division, in response to French Resistance actions directed at them, entered Oradour-sur-Glane and took out their

---

167 Bradley, *A General's Life*, 234.

frustrations on the population. The shooting did not end until 6 p.m., after 642 people were murdered and the town set ablaze. Remarkably, some of the SS who took part in the atrocity were themselves Frenchmen, Alsatians recruited by the SS in Alsace.[168]

LANDING

At 1:30 am on D-Day June 6, 1944, on Montgomery's right, the U.S. 101st Airborne Division began landing by airborne insertion southeast of Ste.-Mère-Église. At the same time, the U.S. 82nd Airborne Division jumped in near the "Utah" beaches. At 2 a.m., the British 6th Airborne Division was dropped in the vicinity of the coastal battery at Merville, on Montgomery's left. Operation Overlord had begun.

At 6:40 a.m., the U.S. 4th Infantry Division landed on Utah Beach. Casualties were moderate, the beachhead was secured, and the troops started moving inland. By the end of the day, elements of the 4th had moved up to 10 kilometers inland and linked up with elements of the 101st Airborne Division. On Omaha Beach, the U.S. 1st Infantry Division landed at 6:34 a.m. and immediately encountered heavy resistance from the German 352nd Division. Most of the amphibious tanks failed to make it to the beach as a result of rough seas and underwater obstacles. For a time, the landing on Omaha was in question. However, the 1st Division's 16th Infantry Regiment, with extreme gallantry, stormed the German positions and gained a foothold on the beach. By sunset, the beachhead was secure and the troops had moved inland.[169]

In the British sector, the 50th Division landed on Gold Beach

---

168 Bradley, *A Soldier's Story*, 270-274.; Max Hastings, *Das Reich: The March of the 2nd SS Panzer Division Through France* (New York: Holt, Rinehart and Winston, 1981), 169-168.; Guy Pauchau and Pierre Masfrand, *Oradour sur Glane, A Vision of Horror* (Oradour-sur-Glane, FR: Association Nationale Des Familles Des Martyers D'Oradour-sur-Glane, 2003), 140.; Ibid., 199.

169 Montgomery, *Normandy to the Baltic*, 42-44.; Bradley, *A Soldier's Story*, 270-274.

on the right, the 3rd Canadian Division on Juno Beach in the center, and the 3rd British Division on Sword Beach on the left. For a while, the 50th Division was pinned down on the beach, but it was eventually able to fight through the resistance. The division reached its day-one objective on the Bayeux-Caen Road and was able to link up with the 3rd Canadian Division but not the U.S. 1st Division on its right. The 3rd Canadian Division also initially faced stiff resistance but was able to fight through it, and achieved one of its two objectives that day. The 3rd British Division was to advance on Caen and establish a bridgehead over the Orne River, which runs through the center of the city. The 3rd Division was unable to accomplish this, though they did fight off an attack of twenty tanks from the 21st Panzer Division. The results for the day were encouraging, even though not all objectives had been taken. One of those untaken objectives was Caen.[170]

The role of the 3rd Canadian Infantry Division has often been misinterpreted by historians, who believed the division was to capture Caen on D-Day. The objectives assigned to the division were to establish a covering position west of Caen to defeat all counterattacks. The British 3rd Infantry Division was to capture Caen on D-Day while the Canadians defended west of the town. Indeed, the divisional boundary between the Canadian and British divisions was two kilometers west of Caen. Though the 3rd Canadian Infantry Division did fail to exploit the absence of strong enemy forces to their front on June 6, in four days of hard combat, June 7 to 11, they did prevent the I SS Panzer Corps from gaining access to the beach. This neutralized the threat of being driven back into the sea by German armor. Hitler himself directed that the German armored attacks were to launch from

---

170   Ibid., 42-44.

the Caen area.[171]

Capturing Caen on D-Day was not outside the realm of feasibility. F.L. Ellis, the British historian, wrote in his *Victory in the West* (2014) that the "failure to capture Caen on D-Day was due partly to the congestion on the beach, partly to the intervention of the 21st Panzer Division intervening at certain points along the way to Caen that day, and partly due to the pace at which the British operations were carried out. Caen was only eight miles from the coast and to seize it on D-Day the British would have to advance as rapidly as possible, and at times, there was little evidence of the sense of urgency required to take Caen that day."

Brigadier Nigel Poett, who commanded the 5th Parachute Brigade, claims Caen could have easily been taken on D-Day. "In the morning, one of my companies could have taken Caen, by afternoon, its capture would have required one of my battalions, and by nightfall, it would have required the whole 6th Airborne Division to take Caen."[172]

Omar Bradley continued, "In sum, the British and Canadian assault forces sat down. They had Caen within their grasp, and they let it slip away, Monty lost the opportunity to have his tanks knock about near Falaise as he had boasted. The new bold Monty of the Saint Paul's schoolroom was gone. The old cautious, methodical Monty was back."[173]

Eisenhower seemed optimistic when he visited Normandy on June 12, even though Caen had not been captured, but by June 20, his demeanor had changed due to the slow progress

---

[171] Marc Milner, "Stopping the Panzers: Reassessing the Role of 3rd Canadian Infantry Division in Normandy, 7-10 June 1944," *The Journal of Military History*, (April 2010), 492-494, accessed December 15, 2015. http://search.proquest.com.ezproxy2.apus.edu/docview/195636835?pq-origsite=summon&accountid=8289.; Warlimont, *Inside Hitler's Headquarters*, 429.

[172] Lamb, *Montgomery in Europe*, 93.

[173] Bradley, *A General's Life*, 254.

of the invasion forces. Given the advantages of air supremacy and access to German plans and combat readiness through Ultra, Eisenhower did not understand why the Germans were not being pushed back. Montgomery was beginning to feel the pressure. As of July 15, 770,000 American soldiers had entered the theater and 73,000 of them had become casualties, and likewise, 591,000 British soldiers had arrived from England, of which 49,000 were wounded or killed. Montgomery's command now consisted of thirty-four Allied divisions.

Field Marshal von Gerd von Rundstedt commanded the German forces in France. Field Marshal Rommel commanded Army Group B, with the Seventh and Fifteenth Armies. The Seventh Army, opposing the Allies in Normandy, controlled six armored divisions and twenty infantry divisions. Rommel could not use the Fifteenth Army in Normandy, as both Hitler and von Rundstedt thought Normandy was a feint and that the actual invasion would come at Calais.[174]

CAEN

Montgomery failed to take Caen on D-Day and, on June 8, he ordered General Dempsey, the Second Army commander, to develop operations with all possible speed for its capture. The next day Montgomery sent the XXX Corps to attack Caen by a swing to the right through Villers-Bocage. Once Villers-Bocage was taken, the British 1st Airborne Division would drop to the south of Caen, and the Americans would support from their positions in Chaumont. The British 7th Armored Division took Villers-Bocage on June 13 but was not able to hold it. Elements of the 2nd SS Panzer and Panzer Lehr Divisions forced the British to withdraw. Montgomery's attempt to encircle Caen from the

---

[174] Richard Overy, *Why the Allies Won* (New York: Norton and Company, 1995), 166.; Steven Ambrose, *Eisenhower: Soldier and President* (New York: Simon and Schuster, 1990), 322.

northwest was a failure. This action, known as the Battle of Chaumont Gap, was Montgomery's first defeat in Normandy.[175]

On June 15, Captain Harry Butcher, Eisenhower's naval aide, wrote in the SHAEF Diary that "Eisenhower was concerned that Montgomery would not be able to attack again until September 17. Eisenhower wanted the Germans kept off balance by a never ending attack. But apparently Montgomery wants to tidy up his administrative tail and get plenty of supplies on hand before he makes a general attack."[176] As it turned out, Montgomery would not conduct any serious attacks in the vicinity of Caen until June 23. On June 18, Montgomery remained focused on the capture of Caen; he issued a directive that day which stated, "It is clear that we must now capture Caen and Cherbourg, as the first step in the full development of our plans. The immediate task of the Second British Army will be to capture Caen. I shall hope to see both Caen and Cherbourg captured by June 24."[177]

Montgomery's next attempt to take Caen, Operation Epsom, took place June 26 to 30, 1944. The British VIII Corps led the attack. The original objectives of Epsom were to capture Caen, cross the Orne River, and take control of the southern approaches to Caen. To shape the battlefield before Epsom, Montgomery conducted several attacks beginning on June 23. I Corps was ordered to fix elements of the 21st Panzer Division into place southwest of Caen. XXX Corps was ordered to secure the high ground on the right of the avenue of approach that VIII Corp was to use in its attack on Caen. When these preliminary attacks were over, the I Corps had succeeded in their mission

---

175 Lamb, Montgomery in Europe, 112-113.
176 Harry Butcher, *My Three Years With Eisenhower: The Personal Diary of Captain Harry C, Butcher, USNR, Naval Aide to General Eisenhower, 1942 to 1945*. (New York: Simon and Schuster, 1946), 501.; Eisenhower, *Crusade in Europe*, 260.
177 Russell Weigley, *Eisenhower's Lieutenants, The Campaign of France and Germany 1944-1945* (Bloomington: Indiana University Press, 1981), 172.

southwest of Caen. However, the XXX Corps was unsuccessful in gaining the high ground they were directed to take.[178]

Operation Epsom kicked off in the early morning of June 26. A typical Montgomery heavy-artillery barrage pounded the Germans while VIII Corps began their advance. Air cover was poor as a result of the weather and did not provide effective support to the British. By the end of the first day, though the objective of crossing the Odon River had not been accomplished, most of the German defenses east and southwest of Caen had been overrun. The next several days of hard fighting resulted in heavy casualties for both the British and the Germans. The British finally crossed the Odon River but could advance no farther against increasing German resistance. Finally, a German counterattack on June 30 forced the British to withdraw from the Odon River, and an additional British attack north of Caen was stopped with heavy British casualties, especially in the infantry. However, in the center, the British and Canadians did succeed in taking the western part of Caen. The British executed the attack only with armor, no infantry. Without infantry to clear out anti-tank guns, British tanks paid a heavy toll for the success. The Germans, however, still retained control of southern Caen and the Bourguebus Ridge south of the city. It was German possession of this key terrain that was the obstacle to a British breakout.

By now, six Panzer Divisions were committed against the British. Montgomery asked Bradley for the loan of the U.S. 3rd Armored Division to use as a reserve. Because of the situation on the First U.S. Army front, Bradley refused. Though as the Army Group commander, Montgomery could have taken the division, he did not press the issue. As a compromise, Bradley agreed to

---

178 Hans Von Luck, *Panzer Commander: The Memoirs of Colonel Hans Von Luck* (New York: Dell, 1978), 188.; Lloyd Clark, Operation Epsom (Gloucestershire, UK: Sutton Publishing, 2004), 21,; Ibid., 27-28,; Ibid., 104-105.

take over a part of the British Second Army front.[179]

In accessing the results of Operation Epsom, one has to confront the confusion caused by uncertainty of what the actual objectives were. The original objectives were to capture Caen, cross the Orne River, and dominate the southern approaches to Caen. These were not obtained. Montgomery, not wanting to add to the tarnish on his reputation after his somewhat lackluster performances in Sicily and Italy, simply changed the original objectives after completion of the operation. The new objectives were to weaken the German position in Normandy and to eliminate the II SS Panzer Corps' threat to Bayeux.[180]

Whatever Montgomery's objectives were, as a result of Operation Epsom, the Germans reinforced the Caen sector, which would make further attempts to take Caen even more difficult. During Epsom, German Lieutenant Colonel Hans von Luck commanded two panzer battalions. After Epsom, he received two additional panzer battalions (one equipped with Tiger tanks), an assault gun battalion, a rocket launcher unit, and an infantry battalion. The Battle Group von Luck now had the combat power of a Panzer Regiment. The Germans also established an anti-tank gun line south of Caen on the Bourguebus Ridge. This gun line used powerful 88-millimeter Flak guns, possibly the best anti-tank weapon of the war.[181]

The Allied leadership began to lose patience with Montgomery. His failure to take Caen dashed British hopes for enlarging the beachhead. The areas southeast of Caen projected for airfields remained in enemy hands, and Montgomery's plan for pivoting on Caen was thus impossible. The Royal Air

---

179 Clark, *Operation Epsom*, 45-49.; Lamb, *Montgomery in Europe*, 115-116.; David Zabecki, *Germany at War: 400 Years of Military History* (Santa Barbara: ABC-CLIO, 2014), 556.; Bradley, A Soldier's Story, 327.
180 Clark, *Operation Epsom*, 104-105.
181 Von Luck, *Panzer Commander*, 189.

Force was furious, especially when Montgomery kept insisting that everything was going according to his plan. Air operations had been planned based on using newly constructed airfields southeast of Caen. Now these airfields had to be built in the congested beachhead, within range of enemy artillery. Room for ammunition, fuel, and food, not to mention soldiers, was rapidly running out. Bradley noted that the British were so overcrowded on their beachhead that they were spilling over onto his.[182]

Churchill and President Roosevelt feared a stalemate was developing in Normandy even as the Russians were pushing the Germans west toward Germany. Politically, the Allies could not afford a stalemate or the appearance of one. Such a situation could provide Hitler the opportunity for a negotiated peace with Stalin, and while this was unlikely, it was a major concern for both Roosevelt and Churchill. Nowhere in Normandy were there any indications of the bold and unexpected thrusts they desired. The American First Army was no closer to breaking out of the beachheads than the British.

This unhappy situation reflected poorly on Montgomery and his generalship. It is significant that, in his memoirs, Montgomery does not even mention Operation Epsom.[183]

BREAKOUT

The Allied breakout of the Normandy beachheads was to occur during Operation Goodwood, executed by the British, and Operation Cobra, executed by the Americans. Ironically, Montgomery, the overall ground commander, did not conceive these operations. He convened a conference on July 10, 1944, which included his two Army Commanders, the Second British Army commander, General Dempsey, and the First U.S.

---
182 Anthony Beevor, *D-Day The Battle for Normandy* (New York: Viking, 2009), 183-185.
183 Mason, *Breakout Drive to the Seine*, 21.; Carlo D'Este, *Decision In Normandy* (New York: E. P. Dutton, 1994), 304.

commander, General Bradley.

Montgomery was worried about preventing an operational stalemate and wanted to discuss options for a breakout. Bradley presented a plan for an American breakout that would give him the maneuvering space he needed to seize the Brittany ports, which were required because of the damage to the Port of Cherbourg. Bradley would coordinate massive airstrikes to create conditions for his breakout. While Dempsey did not yet have a plan, he wanted to execute a breakout as well. Dempsey believed that a breakout attempt by the British just before the American breakout would draw Germans away from the Americans and facilitate the second breakout. Montgomery approved both presentations. The British breakout attempt was called Operation Goodwood; the American attempt was labeled Operation Cobra.[184]

Until his death, Montgomery claimed it was his concept to draw the German armor away from the First Army and onto the Second Army to facilitate Bradley's breakout. It was Dempsey, not Montgomery, who foresaw this, but then, Montgomery was notorious for claiming the credit for his subordinates' ideas. For the Second Army breakout, Montgomery directed Dempsey to develop a plan "for a massive stroke from Caen toward Falaise."[185] Operation Goodwood, to be executed on July 18, 1944, would include the British XII and VIII Corps and the Canadian II Corps. The XIII Corps was designated the main effort and was to seize the plain to the southeast of Caen and advance toward Falaise. The II Corps was to take southern Caen, and the XII Corps was to conduct a diversion southwest of Caen. The British allocated 1,200 tanks to the operation; the Germans had only 277 tanks. On July 17, General Montgomery assured Eisenhower

---

184 Martin Blumenson, *Breakout and Pursuit* (Washington D.C.: Center of Military History United States Army, 1984), 187-188.; Bradley, *A General's Life*. 272.
185 Zabecki, *Germany at War*, 557.

that "my whole eastern flank will burst into flames and that in a bold stroke will result in a decisive victory that will knock loose our present shackles."[186]

Eisenhower believed all of Montgomery's pronouncements on Operation Goodwood. Goodwood would also provide space needed for logistical assets and the airfields the Allied Air Forces required. Montgomery had requested massive air support for Goodwood, both bombing and ground attack missions.

Operation Goodwood started at 5:30 a.m. on July 18, 1944, with bombing missions to suppress a corridor that would allow passage of the attacking British. Allied intelligence analysts believed the German defenses were seven kilometers deep, so the air attack plan directed carpet bombing to a depth of seven kilometers. Unknown to the Allies, the German defense was fifteen kilometers deep. In the rear of this defensive sector, the Germans had placed their new anti-tank line, on Bourguebus Ridge, after Operation Epsom. The bombing left this line untouched.[187]

At 7:45 a.m. the British VIII Corps began its attack and made good progress because the Germans were still dazed from the bombing. The bombing had succeeded in destroying much of the German defensives within the seven-kilometer zone. The British advanced three kilometers in the first three hours. By 1:00 p.m., VIII Corps was at the base of the Bourguebus Ridge, where the German 88s began opening up on the British. The British loss of tanks brought the advance to a halt. Lieutenant General O'Conner, the VIII Corps commander, immediately notified Montgomery and kept him updated throughout the afternoon.[188]

At 2:00 p.m., knowing full well the attack had stalled,

---

[186] Blumenson, *The Battle of the Generals*, 117.; Bradley, *A General's Life*. 273.
[187] Von Luck, *Panzer Commander*, 189.
[188] D'Este, *Decision at Normandy*, 374-381.; John Keegan, *Six Armies in Normandy: From D-Day to the Liberation of Paris June 6th – August 25th, 1944* (New York: Viking Press, 1982), 216-217.; Blumenson, *Breakout and Pursuit*, 193.

Montgomery sent a message to the Chief of the Imperial General Staff, Alanbrooke, saying, "The situation is very promising and very few enemy tanks have been encountered." He also had his Public Affairs Officer issue a release stating, "Early this morning British and Canadian troops attacked and broke through east of the Orne River and southeast of Caen. Heavy fighting continues, General Montgomery is well satisfied with the progress made in the first day's fighting of this battle." The next morning the *London Times* proclaimed in print, "Second Army Breaks Through—Armored Forces Reach Open Country—General Montgomery Well Satisfied."[189] That day, not only had the attack been stopped, but the British had lost 270 tanks and sustained 1,500 casualties.

On July 19, the British continued the attack but made little progress. Eisenhower was pressing Montgomery for his objectives: he wanted to know if Operation Goodwood was a breakout attempt or not. Montgomery told General Dempsey, "There is no need to tell Ike anything." Montgomery was keeping his objectives vague, just like during Operation Epsom. If the breakout attempt was successful, he would claim the credit, if not he would say his objective was simply to tie down German forces to assist the American breakout.[190]

During the afternoon of July 20, a severe thunderstorm broke out. The ground turned into a sea of mud, ending any hopes of continuing the attack, and the operation was called off. Operation Goodwood had pushed the Germans back six miles in the south, three miles in the east, and the Germans had finally withdrawn from Caen, but Montgomery had not achieved a breakout in the east. The Germans had delayed Montgomery for almost five weeks in his drive to take Caen; now he had

---

189 Wilmot, *The Struggle for Europe*, 360.
190 Beevor, *D-Day*, 229.

finally taken it. But it was at a high cost. Operation Goodwood produced four thousand British casualties, and five hundred tanks were lost. He could replenish the tanks easily enough—the Americans would see to that—but the losses in men would be difficult to make up.[191]

Marshall was not satisfied with Montgomery's progress on the eastern side of the Normandy beachhead. On August 2, Eisenhower had to defend Montgomery in a top secret cable to Marshall. He accepted the responsibility for the delays, telling Marshall Montgomery's activities had performed a containing action while the Americans were securing Cherbourg. He admitted that the first objective of the operations around Caen was to secure it and use the favorable terrain there for a breakthrough. Though the breakthrough had failed, he reiterated that the containing action was successful. Eisenhower might have mollified Marshall, but the successful breakout by Bradley's First Army in Operation Cobra certainly must have mollified him further.[192]

Operation Epson and now Goodwood had been failures resulting in heavy casualties. Operation Goodwood had finally given Montgomery Caen, but the breakout of the British Army still eluded him. Instead of accepting the responsibility for these failures like a true professional, he heaped all the blame on the commanders of the 51st Highland Division, the 50th Northumbrian Division, and the famous 7th Armored Division. These proud divisions had to undergo the humiliation of being pulled out of the line and having their commanders relieved of duty.[193]

Montgomery later attempted to pretend that operations in Normandy went entirely as he had planned. According to his plan, the British were to pivot on their left at Caen and defend

---

191 Blumenson, *Breakout and Pursuit*, 193.; Ruge, *Rommel in Normandy*, 215.
192 Chandler, ed, *The Papers of Dwight David Eisenhower*, 2048-2049.
193 Delaforce, *Monty's Highlanders*, 141.

against enemy attacks from the east toward the lodgment area. Montgomery made clear that the strong front would be somewhere in the vicinity of Falaise. Montgomery distorted the facts after the failure to take Caen by insisting that he accomplished this by holding a line north of it. Maintaining the strong line near Falaise was to provide adequate room for troop and supply buildup as well as for the construction of airfields between the coast and the perimeter. Without it, the Allies suffered greatly from lack of space within the beachhead and lack of airfields, leading to lack of adequate tactical air support.

All who knew Montgomery and his plan, especially the Americans, were not fooled by his deceptions when his plans failed. Had he been forthright and less arrogant about his difficult situation on his left, the discontent directed at him might have been significantly reduced. Yet he consistently claimed that all his campaigns went exactly according to his plans.

Montgomery's delay in taking Caen greatly disappointed Eisenhower. The reputation he had won at Second Alamein and so zealously guarded was undoubtedly enhanced by Operation Overlord. However, it had taken a beating over Caen. The false report he sent to Alanbrooke, as well as the lying press release, both on July 18, also reflected poorly on his integrity.[194]

FALAISE

Immediately after the success of Operation Cobra, Patton's Third Army made rapid advances to the south and southwest. Both Montgomery and Bradley saw the potential to envelop the German forces south of the Seine River. Still in command of Allied ground forces, Montgomery planned a British advance toward Falaise to cut off and surround German Army Group B,

---

194   Max Hastings, *Overlord: D-Day and the Battle for Normandy* (New York: Simon and Schuster, 1984), 37-38.

which consisted of the Fifth Panzer Army and the Seventh Army. Fearing these forces would be cut off, Field Marshal Gunter von Kluge, commanding Army Group B, requested permission from Hitler to withdraw them to the Seine River. Hitler, who did not entirely trust von Kluge and had taken control of strategy on the western front, forbade any withdrawal. Instead, Hitler ordered von Kluge to counterattack in the direction of Mortain. Hitler allocated seven new divisions to the counterattack from the German Fifteenth Army and southern France. Christened Operation Luttich, the counterattack indicated that Hitler would decide the fate of France, not on the Seine River, but at Mortain.[195]

On August 7, 1944, the German offensive began, and that night the First Canadian Army launched Operation Totalize, their attack on Falaise. The Canadian II Corps led the attack and consisted of two armored divisions, one of them Polish; two armored brigades; and three infantry divisions. Montgomery had insisted upon a heavy bombardment before the attack, and as at Caen, there were some negative results. The operation began with a thousand-bomber raid that softened up the German defenses in front of the Canadians, and unfortunately, destroyed countless villages that had existed for centuries. The bombing had the desired effect on the Germans, but it also turned the ground the Canadians had to traverse into a lunar landscape. Many tanks got stuck in the bottom of bomb craters. Those tanks that identified a crater and stopped to avoid driving into it were often struck by a following tank. Confusion reigned in the darkness, just as it had during the breakout at Second Alamein. Adding to the uncertainty in the early morning hours, the Canadians lost their capability to communicate with each other for several minutes while a master station broadcast a motivational message from Montgomery. Not only was this an

---

[195] Montgomery, *Normandy to the Baltic*, 98-99.; Bradley, *A General's Life*, 295.

inopportune time, but the Canadians knew that at this hour, Montgomery was asleep in his caravan. However, the Canadians and Poles continued their advance, and in the first twenty-four hours, they covered six miles and got within twelve miles of Falaise.[196]

The next day, Bradley decided to change Patton's mission and directed him to send his XV Corps, commanded by Major General Wade Haislip, in the direction of Argentan. Though the Canadian attack toward Falaise had slowed down because of German resistance, Montgomery agreed with Bradley's actions, and assured him that the Canadians would shortly take Falaise and be in Argentan before XV Corp arrived there. Therefore, a new army group boundary was designated, running through Argentan; 21st Army Group north of the boundary line, 12th Army Group south of it. Bradley also established Alencon, just south of Argentan, as the XV Corps' objective. Montgomery believed the only option left to the Germans in the pocket was to fight a delaying action to allow as many to escape as possible. Therefore, he developed a plan to swing the right of the 12th Army Group toward Paris and at the same time to have the First Canadian Army move south toward Falaise. These two pincers would cut off the retreating Germans.

While Montgomery agreed with this short envelopment at Falaise, he also wanted to execute a larger one toward Paris and the Seine River. It was for this longer envelopment that he was saving the Second British Army. While the Canadians were attacking toward Falaise, the Second Army was recuperating and replenishing material after the fighting they went through

---

196   Bradley, *A General's Life*, 293.; Ken Tout, *A Fine Night For Tanks: The Road to Falaise* (Gloucestershire, UK: Sutton Publishing, 2002), 3-6.; Ibid., 14.

during Operation Goodwood.[197]

By August 9, the First U.S. Army, now commanded by Lieutenant General Courtney Hodges, stopped the German counterattack toward Mortain and were attacking the German front. Also that day, the Canadian attack bogged down eight miles from Falaise. The Canadian commander, General Crerar, relieved the Canadian 4th Armored Division commander because he was not advancing fast enough. Patton, knowing that Argentan was within the U.S. boundary, authorized XV Corps to advance past Alencon, and established a new XV objective just south of Argentan. On August 12, while the Canadians were still plodding toward Falaise against stiff German resistance, Haislip's XV Corps secured Alencon. Haislip requested permission to advance to Argentan, and Patton approved the request. Haislip believed he could hold a solid shoulder between Argentan and Alencon. The Canadians, however, were not making much progress, and Patton feared the envelopment would not be completed and that the retreating Germans would escape through the gap between XV Corps and the First Canadian Army. He, therefore, ordered Haislip to advance his XV Corps north of Argentan, across the Army Group boundary to Falaise and, if the Canadians were not there, to push on slowly northward until contact was made with them. XV Corps encountered German resistance as they were advancing toward Argentan; meanwhile, the Canadians were still six miles short of Falaise.[198]

On the morning of August 13, Bradley became aware of

---

[197] Bradley, *A General's Life*, 295.; De Guingand, *Operation Victory*, 407. Martin Blumenson, "General Bradley's Decision at Argentan, 1944." *Command Decisions*, ed. Kent Greenfield (New York: Harcourt, Brace and Company, 1959), 305-306.

[198] Major William Sylvan and Captain Francis Smith, *Normandy to Victory: The War Diary of General Courtney Hodges and the First U.S. Army* (Lexington: University Press of Kentucky, 2008), 90-91.; Martin Blumenson, "General Bradley's Decision at Argentan, 1944," in *Command Decisions* edited by Kent Greenfield, (New York: Harcourt, Brace and Company, 1959), 309-310. , Bradley, A Generals Life, 302.

Patton's actions. He did not think XV Corps could hold the shoulder by themselves. Indeed, the previous night, he had directed Major General Joe Collins to move his VII Corps toward Alencon to reinforce XV Corps.[199] Bradley later wrote, "I had a sharp telephone exchange with Patton. He further infuriated me with his boastful, supercilious attitude. He said let me go on to Falaise and we'll drive the British back into the sea for another Dunkirk. I replied coldly and firmly, nothing doing. You are not to go beyond Argentan. Just stop and build up on the shoulder. I much preferred a solid shoulder at Argentan to the possibility of a broken neck at Falaise."[200] Bradley felt that the capture of Falaise was a matter of prestige to the British, and if Patton took Falaise, it would be a slap in their face. So Patton recalled XV Corps to Argentan, the gap stayed open. The Germans continued to withdraw forces through the gap. However, very few vehicles or artillery escaped.

The Canadians finally arrived at Falaise on August 17, unlike Haislip's XV Corps, they had to fight every for every mile to get there. Realizing there was still an opportunity to close the Gap, Montgomery directed the Canadians southeast to Trun and on to Chambois. Upon a request from Montgomery, Bradley sent Major General Leonard Gerow's Provisional Corps to Chambois, and there the gap was finally closed on August 21, 1944. The Canadians and Poles had advanced nine miles into enemy territory, and they considered this a victory compared to Operations Epsom and Goodwood. The results might have disappointed Montgomery, but the Canadians, not always his biggest admirers, thought he had "exaggerated and unwise expectations" about the operation. In the end, perhaps up to 40,000 Germans escaped through the gap to fight again.[201]

---

199 Blumenson, *Decision at Argentan*, 310-311.
200 Bradley, *A General's Life*, 298-299.
201 Tout, *A Fine Night For Tanks*, 132-133.; *Bradley, A General's Life*, 303-304.

Why did the attempt to close the gap at Falaise fail? It was a brilliant concept, and Montgomery claimed credit for conceiving of the idea for a northward swing by elements of 12th Army Group toward Argentan. However, Bradley claimed it was his idea, writing "Let me put it very plainly: it was my idea. Martin Blumenson credits me as the author. So does Ike."

Montgomery blamed General Henry Crerar, commander of the First Canadian Army, but he never directed any blame toward Bradley or Patton. Bradley however, placed the blame directly on Montgomery. Bradley claimed that instead of leading the Second Canadian Army toward Chambois, he should have kept them moving to Falaise so the gap could be closed there. Montgomery's Chief of Staff laid some of the blame at Montgomery's feet for imposing restrictions, the Army Group boundary, on Bradley. However, it was Bradley who drew this boundary through Argentan; Montgomery just agreed to it. At no time did Bradley ever request a change in the boundary, nor did he request permission for Patton's forces to cross it. It is obvious that it was Bradley's decision to stop Patton at Argentan that caused the failure to close the gap. Bradley's claim that Haislip's XV Corps did not have the combat strength to close the gap and keep it closed is also somewhat questionable, as he had already ordered Collins' VII to reinforce Haislip. Sometimes generals make mistakes. Montgomery would make perhaps the most crucial mistake of the war the following month at Antwerp; Patton made a mistake when he sent Task Force Baum to Hammelberg; Bradley made his biggest mistake at Argentan.[202]

The closing of the Falaise gap at Chambois was the end of the Normandy campaign. From June 6 to August 21, the Germans lost 450,000 men; 210,000 of these were enemy prisoners of

---

202 Montgomery, *Normandy to the Baltic*, 98-99.; Bradley, *A General's Life*, 295.; Blumenson, *Decision at Argentan*, 314; Bradley, *A Soldier's Story*, 376-377.; De Guingand, *Operation Victory*, 407.

war. The Germans also lost more than twenty generals, including Rommel, severely wounded in a strafing attack on July 17. The Germans also lost 1,500 tanks and 3,500 artillery pieces. The Allies sustained 209,672 casualties, of which 36,976 were killed.[203]

---

[203] Alistair Horne, "In Defense of Montgomery," in *No End Save Victory: Perspectives on World War II* ed., Robert Crowley (New York: Putnam's Sons, 2001), 486-487.

CHAPTER VII:
ANTWERP

CAPTURE AND FAILURE TO EXPLOIT

With the failure of the German Mortain offensive and the closure of the Falaise Gap at Chamois on August 21, 1944, the Germans were on the run, and it was a time of pursuit for the Allies. As the Allies approached the Seine River and beyond, Eisenhower realized the "over the beach" method of resupply would shortly become unfeasible. If the Germans could not halt the Allied advance, Eisenhower felt, the overstraining of the logistical system then in place surely would. He began to look at several potential port facilities in the north, all of which the Germans still held. His primary option was the capture and use of Antwerp. Antwerp was the largest port in Europe, and its location, well forward toward the German border, would greatly reduce the Allies' rail and truck haulage requirements. With Antwerp supporting the Allies, logistics would no longer be the primary limiting factor on Allied operations. Also, an offensive in its direction would clear the area from which V-1 and V-2 rockets were launching toward London.[204]

On August 24, Eisenhower gave the mission to capture and open the deepwater Port of Antwerp to the 21st Army Group. He directed Montgomery to "move quickly in order to secure a line that would adequately cover Antwerp."[205] On August 26, while he was still the overall Ground Commander, Montgomery issued orders for the conduct of Allied operations north of the Seine River. In these orders, he stated the immediate tasks confronting 21st Army Group were the destruction of German forces in northeast France, clearance of the Pas de Calais and V-bomb launching sites, the capture of Belgium airfields, and the opening of the Port of Antwerp. He gave the First Canadian Army the task of clearing the French coast and all of the ports to include the Port of Antwerp.[206]

Montgomery told Eisenhower the quickest way of opening the Port of Antwerp was to place the majority of combat power on the left under him. Eisenhower agreed, but then Montgomery asked for an American Army of twelve divisions. Eisenhower replied that this would leave the 12th Army Group with only one army in it, and this he refused to do. However, Eisenhower made Montgomery's drive to Antwerp a priority and directed Bradley to support Montgomery with his First Army. He also cut the Third Army's logistical support and redirected it to Montgomery.[207]

On August 27, the First Canadian Army crossed the Seine River and drove north. They liberated Rouen on August 30,

---

[204] Eisenhower, *Crusade in Europe*, 290-292.
[205] Chandler, ed., *The Papers of Dwight David Eisenhower*, 2090.
[206] Montgomery, *Normandy to the Baltic*, 123.; Eisenhower, *Crusade in Europe*, 293-294.; Mark Zuehlke, *Terrible Victory: First Canadian Army and the Scheldt Estuary Campaign: September 13 – November 6, 1944* (Vancouver: Douglas and McIntyre, 2007), 35.
[207] Montgomery. *Memoirs*, 240.; Wilmot, *The Struggle for Europe*, 468.

reached and bypassed Lille by September 2, and by September 3 brushed aside all German resistance south of Tournai, where they remained overnight. Montgomery was demonstrating that he too could conduct a pursuit.[208]

On September 4, 1944, the 11th British Armored Division, currently under the control of the First Canadian Army, captured Antwerp. At the same time, Eugene Colson and a group of his Belgian Resistance fighters captured the port facilities and two of the three bridges over the Albert Canal. The 11th Armored Division took control of the port facilities, which had only minor damage. That evening, Montgomery telegraphed Eisenhower that the time had come to make a single, powerful drive on Berlin.

Eisenhower replied with a directive with the missions for each army group.[209] To Montgomery, he directed, "The mission of the Northern Group of Armies (21st Army Group), is to secure Antwerp, breach the sector of the Siegfried Line covering the Ruhr, and then seize the Ruhr."[210] On September 5, Eisenhower wrote Montgomery once more, but this time for his eyes only. "While agreeing with your conception of a powerful and full-blooded thrust toward Berlin, I do not agree that it should be initiated at this moment to the exclusion of all other maneuver. While we are advancing we will be opening the ports of Havre and Antwerp, which will be essential to sustain a power thrust deep into Germany. No re-allocation of our present resources would be adequate to sustain a thrust to Berlin."[211]

On September 5, the 11th Division drove toward one of the bridges on the Albert Canal, which was still held by the Germans. On the way they encountered Eugene Colson, who pleaded with the British to take the bridge, but the British

---
208 Montgomery, *Normandy to the Baltic*, 123.
209 Zuehlke, *Terrible Victory*, 35 - 36.; Wilmot, *The Struggle for Europe*, 483.
210 Chandler, ed, *The Papers of Dwight David Eisenhower*, 2116.
211 Ibid., 2120.

declined. Nor would they provide any assistance to the Belgians securing the other two bridges. Major General George (Pip) Roberts, the Division commander, was not willing to execute any task that did not come from his chain of command; this was the way things were done in Montgomery's Command. As the British tanks drove away from the canal, the Belgians yelled, "Goddamn you Britishers, goddamn you." Colson was able to hold the bridges they had taken the day before for only a short time against German attempts to retake them. The British finally realized these bridges would be vital if any additional orders to continue the advance were received. However, death came to the Belgian defenders before the British came to their senses.[212]

The Germans captured the two bridges held by the Belgian resistance on September 6. They secured them for two reasons, to prevent their use by the Allies and for the remnants of the German Fifteenth Army south of the Albert Canal to rejoin their units north of it. The Port of Antwerp had been taken, but it was not opened. The intent for the 21st Army Group attack to the north was to capture and open a deepwater port. The logistical buildup could then use that port to support future offensive operations on the other side of the Rhine. This was not accomplished.[213]

Part of the failure of the 11th Armored Division to attack over the Albert Canal on September 5 or 6 was the result of the poor dissemination of intelligence in 21st Army Group. Information about the disposition of the Fifteenth German Army apparently remained at the Army Group Headquarters. Antwerp, as a supply port, depended as much upon the control of the seaward approaches as upon possession of the harbor itself. Nowhere in Montgomery's directive of August 26, 1944 is there any mention of these approaches.

---

212 Zuehlke, *Terrible Victory*, 37.
213 Zuehlke, *Terrible Victory*, 38.; Wilmot, *The Struggle for Europe*, 483

If Montgomery did not know the military value of the Scheldt Estuary, Hitler certainly did. On September 3, Hitler recognized the threat to Antwerp and ordered Army Group B to hold the Scheldt Estuary by defending Walcheren Island and Flushing Harbor. This message was intercepted and decoded through Ultra and was in Montgomery's hands on September 5. Montgomery also received an Ultra message concerning Hitler's order of September 7 to the Fifteenth Army to deny the Allies use of the Port of Antwerp for as long as possible by occupying both banks of the Scheldt Estuary and defending Walcheren and the area around Breskens.[214]

Lieutenant General Horrocks, the British XXX Corps Commander, said later that if he had known the disposition of the German Fifteenth Army, he would have attacked over the Albert Canal and cut off the Breveland Isthmus. Had he done this, the Fifteenth Army would have been unable to occupy the Scheldt Estuary, and it might have even been destroyed as a fighting force.[215] Horrocks further stated, "My eyes were fixed entirely on the Rhine, and everything else seemed of subsidiary importance. It never entered my head that the Scheldt would be mined, and then we would not be able to use Antwerp Port until the channel was swept and the Germans cleared from the coastline on either side."[216]

While Horrocks gallantly assumed the responsibility for this error, Montgomery, as the Commander, cannot be found faultless. Horrocks, a very professional officer, focused upon what his commander focused upon. Montgomery himself failed to appreciate the key terrain around Antwerp. He saw only the port, not the estuary leading to it. He certainly did not realize that without the estuary, the port was useless.

---

214 Lamb, *Montgomery in Europe*, 212.; Ralph Bennett, *Ultra in the West: The Normandy Campaign 1944-1945* (New York: Schribner's Sons, 1979), 147-148.
215 Zuehlke, *Terrible Victory*, 46-48.
216 Horrocks, *A Full Life*, 204.

Montgomery failed to understand that he had not completed his mission at Antwerp. He was directed to open its port. He knew the port was required to support any significant operation on the far side of the Rhine. However, he made no attempt to correct the situation. What mattered to him now was being the first over the Rhine. He completely disregarded the fact that conditions for successful operations across the Rhine had not been met. And it was he who failed to meet them. Perhaps because he was fed up with Montgomery, Eisenhower revealed the implications of Montgomery's failure to clear the Scheldt Estuary in a cable to the Combined Chiefs of Staff on September 9. Eisenhower explained, "The hostile occupation in force of the islands at the mouth of the Scheldt is certain to delay the utilization of Antwerp as a port and thus will vitally influence the full development of our strategy."[217]

After taking Antwerp, Montgomery committed two tactical errors that had strategic consequences, and once again he failed to exploit his opportunities. Upon taking Antwerp, he should have directed Horrocks' XXX Corps to continue to the Rhine in a pursuit without pause. The retreating German Fifteenth Army would not have had time to reestablish itself into an effective defense and Horrocks might have been able to bounce the Rhine, eliminating any need for the costly and futile Operation Market Garden. Second, Montgomery failed to clear the Scheldt Estuary, which allowed the Germans to deny the use of the Port of Antwerp to the Allies.[218]

With Antwerp taken but useless, Montgomery began pressing Eisenhower for resources for an operation that would put his forces over the Rhine. Obviously, clearing the Scheldt Estuary immediately after capturing Antwerp would have taken time,

---

217 Chandler, ed, *The Papers of Dwight David Eisenhower*, 2124.
218 Bradley, *A General's Life*, 319.

and Montgomery was impatient to launch his drive to get over the Rhine before the Americans did. Time was of the essence in his bid to be the first to reach Berlin. Montgomery wanted Eisenhower to approve Operation Market Garden, but he had done nothing about the blocked Scheldt Estuary. Eisenhower was letting valuable time slip away as well, by not specifically ordering Montgomery to clear the Scheldt Estuary.

Montgomery agreed with Eisenhower that future operations across the Rhine were impossible without an operational Port of Antwerp. However, he did not have the resources to clear the Scheldt Estuary and attack to seize a crossing over the Rhine at the same time. Therefore, he made a deliberate decision to defer clearing the Scheldt Estuary in order to carry out Operation Market Garden, which, even if successful, would have gone nowhere until Antwerp was operational. He would indeed allocate the mission of clearing the Scheldt Estuary to a combat unit, but he would not resource it properly. He would hoard troops and supplies to conduct another operation (Market Garden) and a possible bold stroke toward Berlin while using most, if not all, of the Allied logistical support to do it. In addition, Eisenhower's decision to change the Allied priority of support to the 21st Army Group for Operation Market Garden resulted in the forced halts of the Third U.S. Army on the Meuse River and the First U.S. Army before the West Wall.[219]

Operation Market Garden, Montgomery's attempt to cross the Rhine September 17 to 25, 1944, was not cheap in resources. The Canadian First Army would have to clear the Scheldt Estuary with no assistance from the British Second Army, as they were preparing for an advance into Germany.[220]

---

219 Arnold, *Hollow Heroes*, 167.; De Guingand, *Operation Victory*. 420-422.
220 Weigley, *Eisenhower's Lieutenants*, 516.

OPENING THE SCHELDT

The German Fifteenth Army left some men to hold the Scheldt, while the remainder escaped to Holland to play a critical role in thwarting future British operations. Ultra fully monitored the German evacuation and sent reports to Eisenhower and Montgomery. The First Canadian Army commander, General Crerar, realized the importance of seizing the Scheldt Estuary, but didn't want to confront Montgomery with his assessment. Brigadier Charles Richardson, one of Montgomery's staff officers, understood Crerar's fear. He noted that during this period, Montgomery grew more aloof, remoter, and even less receptive to advice and counsel.[221]

Montgomery's assigned the mission to the First Canadian Army on September 13, 1944. He directed that, in addition to clearing the Scheldt Estuary and opening the Port of Antwerp, they also capture Boulogne, Dunkirk, and Calais. Montgomery expected the Canadians to accomplish these missions simultaneously and with only one corps. The I British Corps, part of the First Canadian Army, was to protect the left of the Second British Army, which was to execute Operation Market Garden along with the First Allied Airborne Army. This left only the II Canadian Corps to accomplish the assigned missions.[222]

Lieutenant General Guy Simonds, in command of the First Canadian Army, conducted his analysis and determined his mission requirements. Simonds recognized that the clearance of the Scheldt Estuary would be a most difficult mission, and the capture of Walcheren Island would be his biggest challenge. Eisenhower sent two American divisions, the 7th Armored Division and the 104th Infantry Division, essentially an American corps, to assist the Canadians. Simonds' plan included the

---
221   Max Hastings, *Armageddon* (New York: Alfred A. Knopf, 2004) 20-22.
222   Jeffery Williams, *The Long Left Flank* (London: Leo Cooper Ltd., 1988), 19-21.

capture of Woensdrecht north of Antwerp; this would prevent additional German forces from entering the Scheldt Estuary. Next he had to clear the Breskens pocket south of the Scheldt Estuary, then South Breveland Peninsula, then the landward approach to Walcheren Island, and finally the island itself. The Scheldt Estuary was heavily defended, and its capture required a major operation, with heavy naval bombardment and concentrated bombing by the Royal Air Force, followed by amphibious and overland operations.[223]

The First Canadian Army began its attack on October 2, 1944. Hampered by driving rain and heavy casualties, they took over two weeks to capture Woensdrecht, finally doing so on October 16, 1944.[224]

Eisenhower did not believe Montgomery was devoting himself enough to the clearance of the Scheldt Estuary. On October 9, he sent a message, "Unless we have Antwerp producing by the middle of November our entire operations will come to a standstill. I consider Antwerp of first importance, and I believe that the operations to clear the entrance require your personal attention."[225] According to Montgomery, it was not until he received this message, over a month after the capture of Antwerp, that clearing the Scheldt Estuary became his immediate objective, and he decided the operation would require all of his resources.[226]

On October 6, Simonds began to clear the Breskens pocket. The fighting raged until November 3, when the south bank of the estuary was finally cleared. In the meantime, the clearance of the South Breveland Peninsula began on October 24 with an

---

[223] Williams, *The Long Left Flank*, 35-40.; Eisenhower, Crusade in Europe, 312.; Butcher, *My Three Years With Eisenhower*, 780.
[224] Williams, *The Long Left Flank*, 111-118.
[225] Chandler, ed, *The Papers of Dwight David Eisenhower*, 2215-2216
[226] Montgomery, *Normandy to the Baltic*, 152.

amphibious assault on the peninsula. Then came the attack on Walcheren Island. By November 9 the estuary had been cleared of enemy forces. Again the cost was high: 27,633 Canadian and British casualties. In the entire Sicily campaign, the Allies sustained 25,000 casualties. Furthermore, the estuary still had to be cleared of mines. The first Allied replenishment ships did not arrive at the Port of Antwerp until November 26, 1944, eighty-three days after its fall.[227]

SUMMARY

"I like to be told by my boss what he wants me to do, and then to be left alone to do it—being given all possible support, but without any interference or fuss," Montgomery would write after the war.[228] This is exactly how Eisenhower dealt with Montgomery over Antwerp. On August 24, he ordered Montgomery to conduct operations to open the Port of Antwerp. He also explained its importance to any Allied operations beyond the Rhine River. If Montgomery had completed a mission analysis, he would have identified the need to secure the Scheldt Estuary along with the port facilities. Historians have suggested Eisenhower needed to give Montgomery a direct order to clear the estuary. To do so insults Montgomery's competence and overstates his professionalism. Montgomery simply put Operation Market Garden, and his desire to be the first over the Rhine River over the Allies' strategic and operational requirements. Time after time, he paid lip service to the necessity of capturing the approaches to Antwerp while denying the men and resources to do this in a timely fashion. The results were disastrous for the Allied campaign. Montgomery did ensure that clearing the Scheldt Estuary was the priority of the First Canadian Army;

---

227 Peter Beale, *The Great Mistake*, (Gloucestershire, UK: Sutton Publishing, 2004), 291-307.; Eisenhower, *Crusade in Europe*, 327.
228 Montgomery, *The Path to Leadership*, 125.

however, within the rest of 21st Army Group, it remained the second priority. There, the planned thrust of the Second British Army to the Ruhr remained the priority. Montgomery obstinately refused to modify his priorities in accordance with his commander's wish.[229]

In his *Normandy to the Baltic,* Montgomery mentions the capture of Antwerp by the 11th Armored Division of XXX Corps. However, he does not speak of the failure to cross the Albert Canal, nor the blunder of not securing the Scheldt Estuary, which would have opened the waterway to the port. Instead, he discusses a two-day halt by XXX Corps to reorganize and to prepare for its relief by XII Corps so it could move northeast to participate in Operation Market Garden. Montgomery was more interested in being the first across the Rhine than opening Antwerp. Jumping the Rhine would be more glorious than clearing the Scheldt Estuary, even though a functioning port at Antwerp was essential to the defeat of Germany.[230]

Had Montgomery cleared the Scheldt promptly, Antwerp could have been included into the logistics scheme much sooner, and the Allies could have avoided the supply nightmare that immobilized them in October. By the time the port was operating, the fall campaigning weather was over, and winter had set in. What of the other consequences that resulted from the delay in beginning operations to clear the Scheldt Estuary? The effects of the weather upon Allied soldiers were more severe. If the attack against the Fifteenth German Army had taken place in early September, the late summer weather would have provided clearer skies, and close air support would have been much more effective. Most of the campaign, perhaps all of it, would have been fought before the fall rains came, lessening the

---

[229] Viscount of Alamein Montgomery, *The Path to Leadership* (London: Collins, 1961), 125.; Hamilton, *Monty: Final Years of the Field Marshal,* 103-106.

[230] Montgomery, *Normandy to the Baltic,* 128.

misery of the soldiers and reducing the wet-weather casualties of trench foot and illness.[231]

By the third week of September 1944, the logistical situation was rapidly heading to a breaking point. The 21st Army Group was finally beginning to clear the Scheldt Estuary and was executing Operation Market Garden; the 12th Army Group and First U.S. Army were attacking at Aachen, attempting to penetrate the German fortifications known as the West Wall, and the Third U.S. Army was expanding the bridgehead east of the Moselle River. At this time, the 21st Army Group was the priority for supply. Both the First and Third U.S. Armies were running short of artillery ammunition and fuel. On September 23, 1944, General Eisenhower informed General Bradley that he was reducing logistical support to the 12th Army Group. The First U.S. Army would receive enough supplies to continue limited attacks in the vicinity of Aachen, but their priority would be to protect the right of 21st Army Group. He also informed Bradley that the Third U.S. Army supplies would be limited to enough to conduct a hasty defense along the Moselle. This meant the Bradley would have to order Patton to stop his pursuit; an angry General Patton had no choice but to comply because of lack of fuel. In effect, because Montgomery had failed to secure the Scheldt Estuary, which could have been done in a few days in early September, the pursuit, one of the most effective American combat operations in history, was called to a halt.[232]

The supplies saved by these measures allowed Montgomery's 21st Army Group to clear the Scheldt Estuary and to resupply and reconstitute the units which participated in the failed Operation Market Garden. It also meant that the German units Patton had pursued now had time to consolidate, reorganize, and establish

---
231 Bradley, *A Soldier's Story*, 425.; Beale, *The Great Mistake*, 303-304.
232 Hugh M. Cole, *The Lorraine Campaign* (Washington D.C.: Center of Military History, 1993), 256-259.

a coherent defense east of the Moselle.

Because of the lack of fuel in the Third U.S. Army, Patton was not able to maneuver to bypass and cut off Metz. He would have to wait until fuel was redirected back to him, which would give the Germans even more time to reinforce Metz, or he would have to conduct frontal attacks on the fortifications west of Metz with little artillery and air support. Patton decided not to wait. He ordered his 5th U.S. Division to attack. The battle for Metz was a bloody struggle which continued until the Germans surrendered on November 22, 1944.[233]

Had the Third U.S. Army been supported with ammunition and fuel, the Battle for Metz might not have ever been fought. The German forces there could have been fixed and bypassed, but supplying the 21st Army Group's operations in and around Antwerp was a higher priority. One might ask why a soldier of Montgomery's stature and reputation would commit such a disastrous unprofessional mistake at Antwerp on September 4 and 5, 1944. The answer is complex. Montgomery won an important victory at Normandy, but his reputation began to tarnish because of a series of setbacks. Montgomery's plan at Normandy called for Caen and the areas suitable for Allied airfields south of it to be captured on June 6, 1944. His initial attempts to take Caen failed. These were followed by Operation Epson, June 26, 1944, which failed to capture Caen[234], and Operation Goodwood, July 18 to 21, which resulted in the capture of Caen but also destroyed what was left of it, fifty-five days later than he estimated it would be taken. Operation Goodwood also failed to achieve a breakout for the British, while the Americans were able to break out as a result of Operation Cobra. Montgomery's attempt to close the Falaise Gap from the

---

[233] Ibid,, 436-449.
[234] Hamilton, *Master of the Battlefield*, 676-680

north also failed, as a result of a decision by Bradley.

Montgomery was also upset because he had been replaced by Eisenhower on September 1, 1944, as the overall Allied Ground Commander.[235] Therefore, he was determined to reestablish his primacy in the battle for Germany. As General David Fraser remarked, "Montgomery's jealousy of Eisenhower affected his decisions at every stage."[236] As a result, his complete attention was on how to get his forces over the Rhine and to Berlin. He cared not at all about opportunities Bradley's Army Group might have, or for that matter, how his failure to secure the Scheldt might affect Allied operations.

Montgomery claimed the halt of XXX Corps was due mainly to lack of fuel that 21st Army Group should have received but was allocated to Patton instead.[237] This does not quite ring true, as XXX Corps had enough fuel to move the sixty miles from Antwerp to its starting position for Operation Market Garden. Even Alanbrooke, Montgomery's leading advocate since they served together in the retreat from Dunkirk in 1940, questioned his failure to advance against the German Fifteenth Army and secure the Scheldt Estuary. Alanbrooke did not do so publicly, continuing to give Montgomery and his military plans the maximum support in public, but in his war diary, he vented his true frustration for the failure to open the port at Antwerp. Alanbrooke's entry for October 5, 1944, reads, "One fact stands out; the Port of Antwerp must be opened with the least possible delay. I feel that Montgomery's strategy for once is at fault. Instead of carrying out the advance on Arnhem he ought to have made certain of Antwerp in the first place. Ike nobly took all blame on himself as he had approved Montgomery suggestion to operate on Arnhem."[238]

---

235   Ibid., 756-763.
236   Hastings, *Armageddon*, 37.
237   Alistair Horne, "In Defense of Montgomery," 490.
238   Alanbrooke, *War Diaries*, 634.

Montgomery felt he needed to do something spectacular to restore his prestige. Opening a port, no matter how critical to Allied operations, did not fit into this category. Getting across the Rhine and driving toward Berlin did. Therefore, while he should have been focused on Antwerp, seizing the opportunities there, and preventing the German Fifteenth Army from occupying the Scheldt Estuary, he was focused on his plan for Operation Market Garden. Faced with the same situation at Antwerp on September 4 to 5, 1944 German Field Marshall Erwin Rommel certainly would have crossed the Albert Canal and cut the Fifteenth German Army from the Scheldt without waiting for permission. Patton would have done the same. Instead, vital time was lost and the war prolonged. Montgomery's failure to do what Rommel and Patton would have done ensured there would be a battle for Metz and a Battle of the Bulge and that thousands of soldiers would die clearing the Scheldt.[239]

---

239 Alistair Horne and David Montgomery, *The Lonely Leader: Monty 1944-45* (London: Macmillan, 1994), 278.

CHAPTER VIII:
OPERATION MARKET GARDEN

PLANNING

Operation Market Garden has both a political and egotistical theme. Though President Roosevelt considered the Soviets trusted allies, Churchill did not. He was concerned about post-war Soviet intentions in Eastern Europe. Churchill recognized the Soviet Union as a mortal danger to the free world and believed the Allies should attempt to deploy forces as far east as possible. Operation Market Garden would be a step in this direction.

Montgomery's reputation was not as stellar as it was after Second Alamein. The long pursuit in North Africa against a vastly inferior foe; the delays in Sicily, Italy, and then taking Caen; and the failure to secure the Port of Antwerp all had their effect. Complaints about Montgomery's generalship were circulating, and Montgomery knew it. Montgomery needed a success, and he needed it quickly so that he could focus on clearing the Scheldt

Estuary. What success could be more spectacular than being the first across the Rhine? Speed was essential here too, as Bradley's 12th Army Group was also trying to get to the Rhine as soon as possible.[240]

The most remarkable aspect of Market Garden was the speed with which the operation was conceived and planned. Montgomery was always a master of methodical planning and preparation. On August 23, at a meeting with Montgomery, Eisenhower made clear that on September 1, he would assume command of Allied ground operations. He went on to affirm he would execute a broad front strategy, and the 21st Army Group would move to open the Port of Antwerp and then on to Germany. Montgomery tried to convince Eisenhower to authorize him to execute a single thrust into Germany. He stated he could get to Berlin and win the war if Eisenhower would guarantee the logistical support.

Eisenhower told Montgomery he could not cut out 12th Army Group and only support Montgomery's Army Group. Montgomery then brought up the V-2 attacks on London, which he knew would strike a chord with Eisenhower because of the importance that Churchill attached to eliminating the V-2 launching sites in the Netherlands. Montgomery proposed a drive into the Netherlands to eradicate these sites using the First Allied Airborne Army. Because of the damage the V-2s were causing in England and the pressure Churchill was putting on Eisenhower, Montgomery knew Eisenhower would be intrigued with the idea, and he was. Eisenhower asked Montgomery to develop a plan, making it clear that this operation would be just an extension of the northern advance to the Rhine. Eisenhower's subordination of the First Allied Airborne Army to Montgomery was a significant gesture,

---

240 Winston S. Churchill, *Triumph and Tragedy* (Boston: Houghton Mifflin Company, 1953), 458.

as it was the Allies' only strategic reserve.[241]

After Eisenhower departed, Montgomery explained his concept to Lieutenant General Frederick Browning, the commander of the I Airborne Corps, part of the First Allied Airborne Army. The plan involved airborne assaults to capture five bridges on the Maas, the Waal, and the Lower Rhine Rivers. These bridges were connected by a single highway, sixty-four miles long, beginning at the Dutch border and culminating at Arnhem. Montgomery told Browning it would take two days for the ground forces to link up with the airborne forces at Arnhem. Browning's opinion was the airborne forces could hold for four days. Montgomery had his airborne component of the operation, and for the ground component, he would use XXX Corps, commanded by his favorite general, Brian Horrocks. He would just have to pull XXX Corps away from Antwerp to get them into position to support Market Garden.[242]

The plan entailed airborne drops to seize the bridges along the main road through Eindhoven to Uden, Grave, Nijmegen, and Arnhem, culminating in establishing a bridgehead north of Arnhem. Horrocks' XXX Corps was to advance along this road to Arnhem, exploit the bridgehead established by the airborne forces, and develop a northern flank on the Zuider Zee and an eastern flank on the Ijssel River. The only drawbacks to the plan were that the drop zones for Arnhem were eight miles from the bridge over the lower Rhine River, and for the plan to be successful, every aspect of it had to work. Every aspect of a plan working in combat is unlikely. The adage that "the plan goes out

---

241 Cornelius Ryan, *A Bridge Too Far* (New York: Simon and Schuster, 1974), 84-87.; Watts, Martin, "Operation Market Garden: Strategic Masterstroke or Battle of Egos?" The Journal of the Historical Association. vol. 98, (April 2013), 191-201, accessed December 12, 2015, http://yw6vq3kb9d.search. serialssolutions.com/?ctx _ver=Z39.88-2004&ctx_enc=info%3Aofi%2Fenc%3AUTF-8&rfr_id=info:sid/summon. 194-195.

242 Ryan, *A Bridge Too Far* (New York: Simon and Schuster, 1974), 88-89.

the window with the first bullet" would prove true for Market Garden. However, if the operation was successful, Montgomery would be the first over the Rhine. Compared to that, all other considerations were minor.[243]

On September 10, 1944, Eisenhower met with Montgomery in Brussels. Most of the meeting was devoted to operations around Antwerp, as that was Eisenhower's priority. Eisenhower was concerned with Walcheren Island, which guarded the mouth of the Scheldt Estuary and was now occupied by elements of the German Fifteenth Army. The most significant consequence of this meeting was Eisenhower's approval of Operation Market Garden. He also made clear to Montgomery that upon completion of Market Garden, he was "to turn instantly and with his whole force to the capture of Walcheren Island and other areas from which the Germans were defending the approaches to Antwerp."[244]

For Montgomery, the short planning cycle was completely uncharacteristic. From the operation's conception, including its planning, to its approval was only sixteen days, and from its approval to its execution was a mere seven days. Montgomery was giving in to his ego: he had to be the first across the Rhine River, and he was going to do something spectacular to repair the damage to his reputation inflicted by Caen and Antwerp.

When Eisenhower approved Market Garden, he was effectively giving Montgomery an opportunity to test his single-thrust theory in a pursuit without pause. This was the right decision. It was, in fact, though Montgomery would deny it, approval for a single-thrust strategy toward the Ruhr, with Patton's Third Army reduced to a supporting effort. If there was to be an early end to the war, it depended on how aggressively Montgomery executed his pursuit without pause. Montgomery's

---
243 Montgomery, *Normandy to the Baltic*, 137.
244 Eisenhower, *Crusade in Europe*, 307.

previous record of mounting such narrow offensives was poor. His single thrust at the Mareth line in March 1943 had ended in disaster, and only De Guingand's concept of a left-hook attack had saved the battle for Montgomery. His plan to take Catania in Sicily by an airborne seizure of a bridge and a narrow armored drive had failed, and he had been forced by circumstances of his own creation to request assistance from Patton to outflank the German defensives in front of him. During this time, neither Montgomery nor Eisenhower was paying the appropriate amount of attention to intelligence. The intelligence showed throughout September that the southern part of the front might yield more quickly to pressure than the northern, that it would be easier to bounce a Rhine crossing up the Mosel or through the Saarland than at Arnhem. However, Montgomery's relentless pressure on Eisenhower to support his operations in the north had its effect, resulting in grave consequences on Allied operations and ending any hope the war would end in 1944.[245]

Intelligence in the planning of Operation Market Garden itself was ignored. On September 10, the Dutch resistance reported that German Panzer units were refitting in Arnhem. A few days later, it identified these units as 9th and 10th SS Panzer Divisions. General Dempsey, the commander of the Second British Army, recommended to Montgomery that the objective be shifted from Arnhem to Wessel. Eisenhower suggested another British or American Airborne Division be dropped on Arnhem to reinforce the British 1st Airborne Division. As was his custom, and as General Marshal had cautioned, Montgomery declined to heed the intelligence reports and the recommendations of

---

245 Bradley, *A General's Life*, 317.; Ralph Bennett, "Ultra and Some Command Decisions," *Journal of Contemporary History*, vol. 16, no. 1, (Jan. 1981), 147, accessed December 13, 2015, http://www.jstor.org.ezproxy2.apus. edu/stable/pdf/260620.pdf?accept-TC=true.; Nigel Hamilton, *Monty: Final Years of the Field Marshal 1944-1976* (New York: McGraw-Hill, 1986), 56.

others; therefore, he refused to change his plan. Montgomery was about to commit one of those errors Marshall had warned Alanbrooke about before the invasion of Italy.[246]

Photographic reconnaissance and Ultra intercepts proved that two or more panzer divisions were near Arnhem. General Bedell Smith, Eisenhower's Chief of Staff, saw these Ultra messages and confronted Montgomery about them. His objections were waved aside by Montgomery. General Brian Horrocks, commander of the British XXX Corps, the ground element of Market Garden, initially called the presence of the two panzer divisions "a bit of bad luck." He claims no one warned him of the possibility of enemy armored assets near Arnhem. Failure to provide Horrocks the information he needed for success on the battlefield was both a moral and professional failure on the part of Montgomery.[247]

The information Ultra provided Montgomery was extraordinary. Ultra informed Montgomery that the 9th and 10th SS Panzer Divisions were between Eindhoven and Arnhem ten days before the launching of Operation Market Garden. On September 14, Ultra informed Montgomery that Army Group B had been headquartered at Oosterbeek on the outskirts of Arnhem. The human intelligence provided by the Dutch underground on September 10 may not have been enough information to modify Montgomery's plan; human intelligence is often untrustworthy or inaccurate. Montgomery was well within his authority as the responsible commander to heed or disregard this intelligence. However, imagery intelligence and Ultra intelligence also indicated armored units near Arnhem. Given these combined reports and Ultra's excellent reliability record from the previous two years, Montgomery's choice is

---

246 Weigley, *Eisenhower's Lieutenants*, 431.
247 Ralph Bennett, *Ultra in the West: The Normandy Campaign 1944-1945* (New York: Schribner's Sons, 1979), 150-151.

less defensible. However, Market Garden was not an operation planned on the tactical situation or opportunities and intelligence about the enemy. There was excessive haste, Anglo-American rivalry, and Montgomery's ego involved. Tanks at Arnhem were an awkward fact that could disrupt Montgomery's plans to bounce the Rhine, so he swept it under the carpet.[248]

Though his plan for Market Garden was approved, Montgomery continued to plague Eisenhower for resources. On September 13, Eisenhower wrote Montgomery that he would get the thousand tons of supplies per day that he required for Operation Market Garden. Air support would deliver five hundred tons, and the other five hundred would come by trucks. Eisenhower also informed Montgomery that providing him this support would immobilize American divisions, but he was willing to do it to enable Montgomery to get across the Rhine and to capture the approaches to Antwerp.[249]

On September 17, Operation Market Garden was launched. The U.S. 101st Airborne Division secured the bridge at Veghel, and the U.S. 82nd Airborne Division secured the bridge over the Maas, at Grave, as well as two bridges over the Maas-Wall Canal between Grave and Nijmegen. However, the 82nd was not able to capture the bridge at Nijmegen due to German resistance, and before the 101st could reach it, the Germans blew the bridge at Son. Though communication with the 1st British Airborne Division at Arnhem was tenuous, it appeared they had secured the north end of the bridge over the Lower Rhine River. At 2:25 p.m., XXX Corps began its advance along the road to Arnhem. The next day, bridging material was on the way to the 101st Airborne Division so it could repair the bridge at Son or construct a new one. At Eindhoven, German resistance was broken at 5:00

---

248   Ibid., 53-54.; Bennett, "Ultra and Some Command Decisions," 145.
249   Chandler, ed, *The Papers of Dwight David Eisenhower*, 2133.

p.m. The 82nd Airborne Division was still fighting its way to the bridge at Nijmegen. Reports from Arnhem were few and far in between, and reinforcements came, but the Germans contained them in the vicinity of the drop zone, eight miles west of the bridge.[250]

On September 19, the weather turned bad, and Montgomery had difficulties getting additional troops dropped at Arnhem. Supply drops to the British in Arnhem repeatedly fell into German hands. The next day, at 6:45 p.m., the 82nd Airborne Division and elements of the Guards Armored Division finally secured the bridge at Nijmegen, and the advance of XXX Corps continued toward Arnhem the next morning. On September 21, German anti-tank guns south of Bessem stopped the British tanks. On September 22, the advance continued, but the Germans cut the route between Uden and Veghel, and it was not reopened until the next day. The Germans cut the route again on September 24. On the morning of September 25, Montgomery decided to withdraw the remnants of the 1st Airborne Division from Arnhem. That night, two thousand survivors of the British 1st Airborne Division were ferried back across the Rhine, but many had to swim the river. Of the 11,900 soldiers of the 1st British Airborne Division committed to Arnhem, 1,485 were killed, and 6,525 were taken prisoner. The division ceased to exist, with the survivors divided up and allocated to other airborne units. The U.S. 82nd Airborne Division had 1,432 killed and wounded, the U.S. 101st Airborne Division 2,118. These casualties combined amounted to a full airborne division. The British XXX, XII, and VIII Corps had a total of 5,264 casualties. In exchange for 16,824 casualties, not to mention all the resources that went into the effort, Montgomery's Market Garden provided the Allies a road that led to nowhere.[251]

---
250 Montgomery, *Normandy to the Baltic*, 139-142.
251 Ibid.,143-146.; Keegan, *The Second World War*, 438.

SUMMARY

Montgomery attributed the failure of Operation Market Garden to bad weather. This was partially true, but as S.L.A. Marshall commented, "This was a convenient way for Montgomery to pass the buck on to God. The student of history might better regard the irreducible fact that the whole plan was as tight as a straitjacket, having almost no margin for error in the calculation of time or space."[252] The battle at Arnhem was the first German victory against the Allied forces since North Africa. Montgomery, driven by his pride, ever concerned with maintaining his reputation, and not willing to accept responsibility for a failure, would always claim Market Garden was not a defeat and that it was 90% successful. The facts do not support his claim.

The British 1st Airborne was the first of the few Allied divisions destroyed in Europe during the war, and all the Allies had to show for their efforts was a salient that led nowhere. The British themselves would bomb and destroy the bridge to prevent its use by the Germans in a potential counterattack in October 1944, and it would not be until late March 1945 that Montgomery would get across the Rhine.

To be sure, the soldiers of the British 1st Airborne Division never felt Market Garden was in any way successful. It led to no anxiety in the Fuhrer Headquarters. Hitler was so confident that the German forces around Arnhem would defeat the British paratroopers that he declined to intervene and allowed the German commanders on the spot to operate as they wished. The Germans were able to defeat Montgomery's operation at Arnhem without disrupting their strategic deployments. None of the formations being assembled for the Ardennes Offensive were distracted from their preparations to fight at Arnhem. The German victory at Arnhem was a much-needed boost for their

---

252 S. L. A. Marshall, Battle at Best (New York: William Morrow and Company, 1963), 8.

morale, and it ensured the war would continue into 1945.[253]

The way Montgomery disregarded solid, confirmed intelligence was not only unprofessional, it verged on incompetent and led to the unnecessary deaths of hundreds of soldiers. General Browning was also on the Ultra list and may have had knowledge of the presence of the 9th and 10th SS Panzer Divisions in the vicinity of Arnhem as early as September 10, for most of the Ultra reports on them were transmitted by September 6. When the imagery intelligence was brought to him by his intelligence officer, Major Urquhart (no relation to the commander of the Airborne Division), Browning told him not to trouble himself over the photographs. This is even more astounding when one considers how easily tanks could overrun the unprotected infantry at Arnhem. However, without the bridge at Arnhem, the whole operation was pointless. This single piece of intelligence clearly held the key to success or failure and, therefore, deserved more consideration than it received. Based on the information available, most of the blame for the intelligence failure can be laid at Browning's feet, but as the responsible commander, a share of the blame must go to Montgomery as well. For him, however, getting across the Rhine River before Bradley was his primary consideration.[254]

Operational miscalculations and tactical errors characterized the planning for Operation Market Garden, and these mistakes contributed greatly to the failure of the mission. Commanders take responsibility not only for their mistakes but the mistakes of their subordinates as well. Eisenhower demonstrated this tenet of military professionalism when he took all blame for the failure of Market Garden upon himself. While Montgomery did admit to mistakes in the planning and execution of Operation

---

253 Walter Warlimont, *Inside Hitler's Headquarters 1939-1945*, 479.; Keegan, *The Second World War*, 438.; Hastings, *Armageddon*, 57.; Lamb, *Montgomery in Europe*, 251
254 Bennett, "Ultra and Some Command Decisions," 146.

Market Garden, he did so only years after the war was over. During the war, his desire to maintain his reputation prohibited him from accepting any responsibility for a failure.[255]

Neither in his postwar writings nor his memoirs does Montgomery admit making a mistake in agreeing to the 1st Parachute Division being dropped eight miles from the objective in two lifts on two days. Regardless of how XXX Corps fared, this decision doomed the British paratroopers. Of the 10,000 soldiers who jumped into the drop zone west of Arnhem, only Frost's battalion of seven hundred made it to the objective. This was not enough combat power to secure the objective, much less hold it until the arrival of XXX Corps.[256]

Instead, in his memoirs, Montgomery wrote, "In my prejudiced view, if the operation had been properly backed from its inception, and given the aircraft, ground forces, and administrative resources necessary for the job it would have succeeded . . . I remain Market Garden's unrepentant advocate."[257] Montgomery's view that Market Garden had been 90% successful is hard to accept. None of the 21st Army Group objectives were met: a bridgehead was not established on the Lower Rhine River, there was no exploitation on the far side of the river, and no V2 launching sites were eliminated.

Prince Bernhard of the Netherlands certainly did not agree with Montgomery's assessment. He commented, "My country can never again afford the luxury of a Montgomery success."[258]

Montgomery's bid for the Rhine and the Ruhr at Arnhem proved nothing less than foolhardy and an expensive waste of

---

255 Steven Semmens, *Decision Making in Alliance Warfare: Operation Market Garden – A Case Study* (Carlisle Barracks, PA.: U.S. Army War College, 2001), 1.; Alanbrooke, *War Diaries*, 600.; Warlimont, *Inside Hitler's Headquarters*, 479.
256 Lamb, *Montgomery in Europe*, 248.
257 Montgomery, *Memoirs*, 267.
258 Arnold, *Hollow Heroes*, 166.

men and materiel. Even if Market Garden had succeeded, would it have been worth it? If a bridgehead had been established north of the Rhine River at Arnhem, it could not have been used for future operations, as the Port of Antwerp was still not open. General Horrocks wrote in his memoirs, "Even if the German panzers had not been in a position to intervene so rapidly, and if we had succeeded in getting right through to the Zuider Zee, could we have kept our lines of communication open? I very much doubt it. In which case instead of XXX Corps fighting to relieve the 1st British Airborne Division, it would then have been a case of the remainder of the Second Army struggling desperately to relieve XXX Corps cut off by the Germans north of Arnhem. Maybe, in the long run, we were lucky."[259]

The responsibility for the failure of Operation Market Garden lies with Montgomery, who should have concentrated his efforts on the less glamorous task of securing the approaches to the Port of Antwerp. Indeed, Operation Market Garden was completely out of character for Montgomery's reputation for caution and overwhelming the enemy with vastly superior combat power. One thing intensified his enthusiasm for the operation: his determination to prove Eisenhower wrong on the narrow-front/broad-front controversy. Success at Arnhem would force Eisenhower to support Montgomery's narrow-front scheme, but it was not to be. In both conception and execution, Operation Market Garden was another great mistake in Montgomery's generalship. As at the Scheldt Estuary, it was an error that prolonged the war.

On April 14, 1945, the Canadian First Army, at last, secured Arnhem—six months after Operation Market Garden, and well after all of the Allied armies were over the Rhine.[260]

---

259 Hamilton, *Monty: Final Years of the Field Marshal*, 89-90.; Horrocks, A Full Life, 231.
260 Royle, *Montgomery: Lessons in Leadership*, 140-141.

CHAPTER IX:
ARDENNES OFFENSIVE

BACKGROUND

By December 1944, the Allies believed the war in the West was almost over. The 6th Army Group, commanded by Lieutenant General Jacob Devers, had closed on the Rhine River in eastern France, and the 12th and 21st Army Groups were knocking on Germany's door. If not for the delay in opening the Port of Antwerp, Bradley and Montgomery might have already crossed the Rhine. Adolf Hitler, knowing the Soviets were planning a great spring offensive, knew he would have to deal with the Allies in the west quickly to stop the Soviet onslaught that was sure to come in a few months. Hitler was aware of the strained relations between the Americans and British, most of it caused by Montgomery. He therefore decided on an operation that could exploit these differences, splitting the American and British Army Groups. Then he could defeat each in detail, capture Antwerp, and negotiate for a separate peace in the west. This would allow the Germans to concentrate all of their combat power in the east. The offensive would emerge from the Ardennes just as it had in 1940.

For the operation, which the Germans dubbed Die Wacht am Rhine, Hitler assembled four armies. The main effort was the Sixth Panzer Army, commanded by SS Oberstgruppenfuhrer Sepp Dietrich. Their primary mission was the capture of Antwerp. The Fifteenth Army, commanded by General Gustav-Adolf von Zangen, had caused Montgomery a great deal of trouble at Antwerp and Arnhem. It was to attack on the right of Sepp Dietrich to fix Allied troops north of the main battle area. The Fifth Panzer Army, commanded by General Hasso von Manteuffel, had the mission to capture Brussels and to protect Dietrich's left. Finally, the Seventh Army, led by General Erich Brandenberger, had the mission to protect the German left flank. For Hitler's plan to succeed, surprise would have to be complete and German progress rapid. Scarcity of fuel required the Germans to move fast and to operate on captured Allied fuel.[261]

THE BATTLE BEGINS

At 5:30 a.m. on December 16, 1944, the German artillery opened up on American units positioned in the Ardennes for rest and recuperation, after being bled white in the Hurtgen Forest. At 6:30 a.m. the artillery ceased, and the Americans witnessed the glow of hundreds of German searchlights as their beams were reflected off the low-flying clouds and back toward the ground to illuminate the battlefield for the attacking panzers and infantry. Initially, the Germans made good progress as they broke through the thin American lines west of the Losheim

---

261 Trevo Dupuy, *Hitler's Last Gamble: The Battle of the Bulge, December 1944 – January 194* (New York: Harper Collins, 1994), 6-7.

Gap. There were annoying delays caused by isolated American units, but as the day went on, the more significant delays were caused by traffic jams, as the Germans attempted to push more combat power toward the west than the transportation infrastructure and terrain could handle. By the end of the first day, Oberstgruppenfuhrer Dietrich was already behind schedule.[262]

The German offensive resumed the next morning, and during the day, the Sixth Panzer Army, spearheaded by Kampfgruppe Peiper, drove as far west as Stavelot. Further south, the Fifth Panzer Army advanced as far west as Poteau and was beginning to isolate St. Vith. It was also on this day, December 17, 1945, that Kampfgruppe Peiper was turned back at Trois Ponts by C Company, 51st Engineers, at the River Ambleve. The brave American engineers blew the bridge over the river in the face of Peiper's panzers. Peiper had to turn back and take up defensive positions around the village of La Gleize. Dietrich's Sixth Panzer Army had made great advances, but as Hitler's main effort, they were beginning to become bogged down, slowed by the tenacious Americans, the terrain, and the lack of fuel. Farther south, von Manteuffel's forces were still making significant gains on December 18 and had reached Bastogne. This beleaguered town, and its subsequent defense by the U.S. 101st Airborne Division, was about to become the focal point of the entire campaign. However, the stubborn American defense of the north shoulder of the salient is what doomed Hitler's dreams of physically splitting the Allies and seizing Antwerp.

Still, Hitler's plan would lead to a change in the Allied command situation that would itself have negative repercussions on the Anglo-American relationship.[263]

---

262 John Toland, *Battle: The Story of the Bulge* (New York: Random House, 1959), 34-35.
263 Ibid. 42-43.; John S. D. Eisenhower, *Bitter Woods* (New York: G. P. Putnam's Sons1969), 261-262.

On December 19, Major General Kenneth Strong, Eisenhower's intelligence officer, assessed that the First U.S. Army would be split by the German advance, which had yet to be stopped by the Americans. He thought it would be best to establish two commands, one to command the units on the northern side of the salient, and one for its south side. He recommended to Eisenhower that Montgomery take command of the units in the north, and Bradley retain command of those in the south. Strong, who was British, did not discuss this recommendation with Montgomery before he presented it to General Bedell Smith, Eisenhower's Chief of Staff. It took some convincing, but Smith finally agreed it was a good idea.

Smith called Bradley to get his opinion. Not surprisingly, Bradley was cool to the idea, but he admitted that it would force Montgomery to commit his reserves to the fight in the Ardennes. The following day, Smith brought up the subject with Eisenhower, who called Bradley with the proposition. Bradley agreed on the issue of the division of command. On December 20, Eisenhower established an army group boundary running on the Meuse River, from Givetto to St. Vith. The U.S. Ninth and First Armies were assigned to the 21st Army Group under Montgomery north of the boundary, leaving Montgomery with just Patton's Third U.S. Army.

The allocation of the U.S. Ninth and First Armies to Montgomery was not an easy command decision for Eisenhower. He was well aware of the animosity both Bradley and Patton, as well as the 12th Army Group staff, held toward Montgomery. However, Eisenhower felt Bradley could not command and control these two armies because of the battlefield environment. Bradley could talk to the two Army commanders by phone, but the face-to-face meetings so essential to effective command were not possible. Chester Wilmot felt that Montgomery believed the defeated Americans had to come to him for him to rescue them from a situation that never would have occurred in the first place, had he remained the overall ground commander.[264]

MONTGOMERY INTERVENES

The German offensive in the Ardennes caught Montgomery by surprise just as much as it did the Americans. On December 15, 1944, Montgomery had written Eisenhower asking for leave so he could spend Christmas with his son. Indeed, Montgomery's daily report for December 16, the very day the Germans initiated offensive mobile warfare in the Ardennes, stated the Germans had not the transport, tanks, or petrol to engage in mobile warfare. Lieutenant General Brian Horrocks was on leave in Belgium visiting the Belgian Royal Family when the German attack began on December 16 and was called back to XXX Corps by Montgomery.[265]

On December 20, 1944, Montgomery took command of both the U.S. First and Ninth Armies. In anticipation of this, he had already Moved XXX Corps to the north of the Meuse River to serve as a backstop for any Germans that succeeded in crossing the Meuse; he also sent reconnaissance troops to cover the bridges over the Meuse. On the morning of December 20, he visited both the First and the Ninth Army headquarters. He allocated some British forces to the Ninth Army and directed Lieutenant General William Simpson to take over part of the First Army line in the north. These British forces saw little, if any, combat in support of the Allied effort in the Ardennes. Montgomery then met with Lieutenant General Courtney Hodges of the First Army. He directed Hodges to form a reserve

---

[264] Hugh Cole, *The Ardennes: The Battle of the Bulge* (Washington DC: Office of the Chief of Military History, 1965), 423-424.; Lamb, *Montgomery in Europe*, 315.

[265] Lamb, *Montgomery in Europe*, 304-305.; Brian Horrocks, *Corps Commander* (Bungay, Suffolk, UK: Magnum Books, 1977), 137-138.

out of VII Corps, commanded by Major General Joe Collins, to be used solely for the Allied counterattack when the time came. Montgomery insisted this reserve consist of four divisions, and that the VII Corps be positioned on the First Army's left.[266]

The divisions on the move to fill out Collins' VII Corps were all American divisions and consisted of the 84th and 75th Infantry Divisions and the 2nd and 3rd Armored Divisions. The U.S. XVIII Airborne Corps, under the command of Lieutenant General Matthew Ridgeway, was also allocated for the counterattack. While Collins liked his new mission, he disagreed that his corps should be placed so far west. Both Collins and Ridgeway repeatedly told Montgomery that VII Corps should be positioned farther east, in the vicinity of St. Vith. They also told Montgomery that his plan for counterattacking at the point, or tip, of the German salient would force the enemy out of the bulge, just as happened during the British Second Army attack at the point of the German salient at Falaise. They insisted the escape route of the Germans needed to be cut near its base. Horrocks was of the same opinion. He too felt that if the Allies had counterattacked further to the east, few if any of their forces would have gotten back to Germany. However, Montgomery was not about to take the advice of American officers junior to him in rank.[267]

Getting VII Corps into position would take a few days, and Montgomery tentatively set the date for the counterattack as December 25. He also gave Collins a direct order not to engage with the Germans until he was ordered by Montgomery to initiate the counterattack. However, an opportunity arose on the battlefield to inflict significant damage to one of Dietrich's best units, the 2nd Panzer Division. On December 23, Collins was briefed by Major General Ernst Harmon, commander of the U.S.

---

[266] Eisenhower, *Bitter Woods*, 261-262.; Montgomery, *Normandy to the Baltic*, 176.
[267] J. Lawton Collins, *Lightening Joe* (Baton Rouge: Louisiana State University Press, 1979), 283-284.; Ibid., 291.; Horrocks, *Corps Commander*, 146.

2nd Armored Division, that elements of the 2nd Panzer Division were near Celles and almost out of fuel. Collins reported this to Hodges at First Army headquarters; unfortunately, Montgomery was there as the report came in. Montgomery directed that plans be made for the defense of the First Army right flank and VII Corps was to hold their positions at all costs. Collins would later say he never received these instructions, so he directed Harmon to prepare an attack on the 2nd Panzer Division. However, on December 24, Collins received directions from Montgomery through the First Army headquarters to go on the defensive. Collins ignored these instructions and, without consulting Montgomery, directed General Harmon's U.S. 2nd Armored Division to attack immediately.

Harmon made his attack on Christmas morning. The battle lasted two days and destroyed almost all the 2nd Panzer Division's armored elements. When Montgomery became aware of VII Corps disregarding his order not to make contact, he directed Horrocks to move the 51st Highland Division as well as the 29th Armored Brigade across the Meuse River to provide additional security. These defensive measures allowed a physical link-up between British forces and the VII Corps. As the mauling of the 2nd Panzer Division was taking place, the U.S. 2nd Armored Division's Reconnaissance Battalion and the British 29th Armored Brigade made contact with the Reconnaissance Battalion of the 2nd Panzer Division. They effectively destroyed it. This encounter was the largest British contribution to Allied combat during the battle.[268]

On December 25, Montgomery wrote Eisenhower that for the Allies to take the initiative, more troops would be needed. He added the only way to accomplish this was by withdrawing from some areas in the salient and shortening the lines. Bradley,

---

268   Ibid., 290.; Eisenhower, *Bitter Woods*, 369-371.

Hodges, and Collins all strongly disagreed with any withdrawals. Collins felt Montgomery put too much stock in the reports of his famous "phantom" observers he sent to the various American headquarters each day. All of these observers were junior British staff officers with little knowledge and even less understanding of how Americans operated. In fact, on Christmas Day, Montgomery had told Bradley that Hodges' U.S. First Army would not be ready to initiate offensive operations for at least three months, that the only attacks possible would be those carried out by Patton's army, and that Patton's army was too weak to have any effect on the Germans. Montgomery went on to recommend to Bradley that he withdraw Patton's forces to the Vosges to gain strength for future attacks. Montgomery's remarks dumbfounded Bradley and disgusted Patton. In reality, Montgomery knew the battle had been won, for much to Horrocks' surprise, Montgomery called him on December 26 and ordered him back to England. Horrocks thought he was being relieved of command; however, Montgomery just wanted him to go home and get some rest for the campaigning that would have to be done after the Germans were defeated in the Ardennes.[269]

Also at this time, Montgomery began to delay the start of the U.S. VII Corps counterattack. After the fight at Celles, and other episodes of enemy offensive activity near the First Army right flank, he did not believe conditions were as yet right for the counteroffensive. His decision to delay the attack from the north greatly angered Bradley and Patton. Both felt he could attack at once if he would use his reserve of four British divisions. This, he refused to do.[270]

Both Collins and Ridgeway disagreed with and were

---

[269] Collins, *Lightening Joe*, 296.; Eisenhower, *Bitter Woods*, 342-343.; Horrocks, *Corps Commander*, 141-142.

[270] Chester Wilmot, *The Struggle for Europe* (Bungay, Suffolk, UK: Richard Clay and Company, 1954), 675.

worried about Montgomery's delay and wanted the VII Corps counterattack launched sooner. Montgomery disagreed. He felt the northern front was not yet stable enough and that this, a traditional tactical concept, was a requirement for the launch. Montgomery also stated that a counterattack in the vicinity of St. Vith could not be supplied along the single road from Liege to St. Vith. Somewhat disrespectfully, Collins replied, "Well, Monty, maybe you British can't, but we can."

Finally, on December 31, 1944, Montgomery agreed to launch the counterattack, with VII Corps attacking in the direction of Houffalize and XVIII Airborne Corps in the direction of St. Vith. However, Montgomery set the date for the attack as January 3, in violation of the agreement he made with Eisenhower to counterattack on January 1, 1945.[271]

The counterattack duly commenced on January 3, and though the weather favored the defense and the Germans fought tenaciously, the lead elements of the VII Corps entered Houffalize on January 15. On January 17, 1945, Patton's forces reached Houffalize from the south. After this junction of forces, the reason for the subordination of the U.S. First Army to the 21st Army Group was no longer valid, and the Army returned to the control of Bradley's 12th Army Group. The U.S. Ninth Army, however, remained under Montgomery. Patton's Third Army continued fighting in the south until January 28, but the Battle of the Bulge was over.[272]

SUMMARY

When Montgomery took command of the northern half of the salient, he rightfully took steps to ensure the Germans would never cross the Meuse by positioning XXX Corps just north

---

271 Collins, *Lightening Joe*, 292.
272 Ibid., 294.

of the river. He also directed the formation of a Ninth Army reserve that would eventually counterattack, in coordination with Patton's Third, and cut the salient at Houffalize. While his actions were correct, his constant desire to withdraw to shorten the line and his delay in launching the VII Corps counterattack rubbed the Americans the wrong way.

General Bradley, not wanting Montgomery to receive too much credit, felt the Americans had interdicted the German breakthrough before Montgomery even took command in the north. Also if it was not for Montgomery's delays in the north, the salient could have been pinched off in the middle, and fewer Germans would have escaped. Evidently, Bradley had learned a lesson from his mistakes at Falaise.

Bradley was not the only one who felt this way. General Collins felt that the Germans suffered a significant defeat in the Ardennes. However, he believed the same results could have been achieved sooner and with even more loss to the Germans if Montgomery had acted boldly. In spite of what Montgomery would later say and write, he did not display confidence in the American soldiers and their leaders; as a result, he unnecessarily prolonged the anxiety of Eisenhower and his staff, as well as the British Chiefs of Staff that the Germans might successfully advance over and beyond the Meuse.

Like Patton, Horrocks believed the Germans were doing the Allies a favor by attacking when they did. Horrocks later wrote, "The Germans were saving us the trouble of a winter offensive across flooded rivers like the Ruhr, the other side of which we would be vulnerable to counterattacks by panzer divisions. Instead, it was the Germans who were vulnerable, and the farther they got, the fewer would get back, we had an opportunity of eliminating much of their armored forces."[273]

Montgomery devotes only seven pages in his memoirs to the Ardennes Offensive. In fact, he wrote, "I think the less one says about this battle the better, for I fancy that whatever I do say will almost certainly be resented."

This concern was brought about by two incidents. First was a letter written by Montgomery on December 29, to Eisenhower, stating "We have had one very definite failure . . . One commander must have powers to direct and control the operation; you cannot possibly do it yourself, and so you would have to nominate someone else." He enclosed a proposed order for Eisenhower to issue to both the 12th and 21st Army Groups directing that "full operational direct, control, and coordination of operations is vested in the 21st Army group commander."

This was beyond even Eisenhower's patience; Montgomery had finally gone too far. Eisenhower asked the Combined Chiefs of Staffs to choose between him or Montgomery. Eisenhower's Chief of Staff, General Bedell Smith, explained this to Montgomery's Chief of Staff, General De Guingand, on December 30, 1944.

De Guingand felt he could straighten the situation out. De Guingand met with Montgomery, who was surprised to find he had driven Eisenhower to such a course. Montgomery immediately wrote a letter containing an apology and a declaration of loyalty. De Guingand quickly returned to Brussels and delivered the letter to Eisenhower, who was mollified. There is little doubt that if De Guingand had not taken these actions, Montgomery would have found himself relieved of command.[274]

The second incident was a press conference given by Montgomery on January 7, 1945. During the press conference,

---

273 Bradley, *A Soldier's Story*, 479-480.; Collins, *Lightening Joe*, 296.; Horrocks, *Corps Commander*, 138.
274 Rich Atkinson, *The Guns at Last Light: The War in Europe, 1944-1945* (New York: Henry Holt and Company, 2013), 473-474.; De Guingand, *Operation Victory*, 434-435.

Montgomery made several comments with which American commanders took issue. He stated that after Eisenhower placed him in command of the northern half of the salient, he employed the whole available power of the 21st Army Group in the battle and that British divisions were fighting hard on the right flank of the U.S. First Army. He added that in fact British divisions were fighting on both sides of the First Army. He called the battle the biggest in the history of the United States Army, one of the most interesting and tricky battles he had ever handled. He also compared the Battle of the Bulge with his first victory, the Battle of Alam Halfa. In fairness, Montgomery also mentioned his admiration for the fighting qualities of the American soldier and his respect for Eisenhower, but the damage had been done. The Americans were irate, especially Bradley, Patton, and Collins. In fact, Collins was indignant at Montgomery's attempts to claim credit for the victory in the Ardennes. Collins wrote, "Monty got under my skin by downgrading the American troops at the time of the Battle of the Bulge . . . however reassuring it was to know Horrocks XXX Corps was backing us up, only one British division ever participated in the fighting. It left a sour note."[275]

---

275   Montgomery, *Memoirs*, 278-271.; Lamb, *Montgomery in Europe*, 332.

CHAPTER X:
CROSSING THE RHINE RIVER

PLANNING

Being first across the Rhine River had been a goal of Montgomery's even before he landed on Normandy. The failed Operation Market Garden was a manifestation of this desire. It was the French First Army that was first among the Allies to reach the Rhine. At 6:30 p.m. on November 19, 1944, the French Moroccan Colonial Infantry Regiment dipped their regimental colors into the Rhine River at Rosenau, France south of Strasbourg. On November 25, the German Garrison Commander of Strasbourg surrendered to the French 2nd Armored Division. The Kiel Bridge over the Rhine was still standing, and the French were anxious to cross. In getting to this position, General De Lattre's French First Army had outflanked the Germans in both Mulhouse and Belfort by their quick maneuvering through the Vosges to reach the Rhine. When the Germans attacked to cut the French off, De Lattre turned the tables on them and took several thousand German prisoners. Russel Weigley wrote, "The First French Army was displaying a boldness of both operational design and tactical execution that Patton could well envy." In the meantime, farther north, the U.S. Seventh Army had reached the Rhine and was preparing to conduct an assault crossing on the present-day Rastatt ferry crossing.[276]

Eisenhower visited General Jacob Devers' 6th Army Group on November 24, and when he discovered Devers was planning a crossing of the Rhine by the French First Army at Strasbourg and the U.S. Seventh Army at Rastatt, he put a stop to it. Eisenhower did not believe he would be able to support Devers' logistical requirements for operations across the Rhine and ordered Devers to halt short of the river. The Germans finally blew up the Kiel Bridge, and eventually, the 6th Army Group would be the last Allied Army Group to cross the Rhine, and ironically the French First Army would be the last army to cross.[277]

Then on March 7, 1945, elements of the 9th Armored Division crossed the Rhine at Remagen, Germany. This time Bradley authorized General Hodges, the U.S. First Army commander, to exploit the crossing. However, this was not an assault crossing, as the famous Bridge at Remagen had been used. Therefore, Montgomery still hoped to be the first to conduct a successful assault crossing of the Rhine, and he intended to cross at Wesel, Germany, when he launched Operation Plunder on March 23, 1945. Unbeknownst to the British, General George Patton's U.S. Third Army had executed an assault crossing of the Rhine at Oppenheim, Germany on March 22, 1945, with elements of the U.S. 5th Division. Much to his and Bradley's delight, Patton

---

[276] Harry Yeide and Mark Stout, *First to the Rhine, The 6th Army Group in World War II* (St. Paul, MN: Zenith, 2007), 238. , Ibid., 254-255.; David Colley, *Decision at Strasbourg* (Annapolis, MD: Naval Institute Press, 2008), 127.; Weigley, *Eisenhower's Lieutenants*, 404.
[277] Colley, *Decision at Strasbourg*, 129-134.

crossed the Rhine the night before Operation Plunder began.[278]

Montgomery initially wanted to execute the crossing at night; however, intelligence indicated that German artillery units in the area could interdict Montgomery's crossing sites once they were identified. This intelligence, along with Montgomery's return to his cautious methods after the failure of Operation Market Garden, would lead to a huge, complicated crossing operation which included an airborne operation to support it. This complexity dictated a daylight operation.

The ground portion of the operation was called Plunder, and the airborne portion Varsity. For Operation Plunder, Montgomery had his organic First Canadian and Second British Armies; he also had the Ninth U.S. Army, commanded by General William Simpson. Altogether, Montgomery had thirty divisions under his command. His plan designated the Second British Army as the main effort, with the Ninth U.S. and the First Canadian Armies in support. He planned to execute an intensive artillery barrage on the far side of the Rhine to suppress the Germans during the crossing operations. This included smoke to obscure enemy observation of the intended crossing sites. Operation Varsity was to occur after the ground phase began, to prevent German artillery from shelling the crossing sites and to interdict any reinforcing moves by the enemy. The primary objective was to capture Wesel, an important transportation hub, similar to Caen. The capture of Wesel would facilitate future 21st Army Group operations in Germany.[279]

The 51st Highland Division was to cross at 9:00 p.m. March 23, in the vicinity of Rees, and establish a bridgehead. The rest of the British XXX Corps would then cross and attack to capture Emmerich and Xanten. The 1st British Commando Brigade

---

278 Collins, *Lightening Joe*, 302-305.; Eisenhower, *Crusade in Europe*, 304.
279 Peter Allen, *One More River: The Rhine Crossings of 1945* (New York: Scribner's Sons, 1980), 210-211.; Montgomery, *Normandy to the Baltic*, 202-203.

was to cross an hour later north of Wesel and to carry out an assault on the city. The First Canadian and the Ninth U.S. were to cross the Rhine in the early morning hours of March 24; the Canadians were to secure the left flank of the Army Group and the Americans the right flank. At 10:00 a.m. Operation Varsity would commence, inserting the 17th U.S. and 6th British Airborne Divisions five kilometers northeast of Wesel to support Operation Plunder. Once the 21st Army Group bridgehead was established and secured, Montgomery planned to construct bridges across the Rhine at Rees, Xanten, Rheinberg, and Wesel. The bridging site at Wesel was the most important because of its proximity to road and rail arteries. Once the bridges were established, the Ninth U.S. Army was to push through its reserve corps to reinforce the Second British Army's breakout into the north German plain.[280]

For weeks, Montgomery had been conducting massive logistics operations, bringing up the engineering and amphibious assets he would need to cross and bridge the Rhine. These assets included resources from both the American and Royal navies. Huge bridging and supply depots, as well as assembly areas for the boats and amphibious vehicles, were established as close to the crossing sites as possible without being detected by the Germans. Hundreds of smoke pots and smoke generators were procured to create a seventy-mile smoke screen along the Rhine to support the crossings. The Soviets would do the same thing when they crossed the Oder River in their drive on Berlin. Montgomery's logistical operations proceeded on schedule.[281]

Montgomery also took steps to isolate the far side of the Rhine. For over a month, the U.S. Army Air Force and the Royal Air Force had been bombing bridges, roads, and rail lines the Germans could use to send reinforcements into the area to oppose the river

---

[280] Allen, *One More River*, 221.; Tim Saunders, *Operation Plunder and Varsity: The British and Canadian Rhine Crossing* (Barnsley, UK: Pen and Sword, 2006), 48-49.
[281] Saunders, *Operation Plunder and Varsity*, 46.

crossings. German airfields, especially those with the Me 262 Jet Fighter, were bombed to keep enemy aircraft grounded. In the month before Operation Plunder, 37,000 tons of munitions were dropped on German targets. Montgomery was leaving nothing to chance. Also, the First Allied Airborne Army, commanded by Lieutenant General Louis Brereton, had to assemble two airborne divisions, the 17th U.S. and 6th British Airborne Divisions, as well as the required lift aircraft and gliders. Indeed, Operation Varsity would be the largest single-day airborne operation in history. By March 23, 1944, all was ready, and at 3:30 p.m. that day, Montgomery ordered Operation Plunder to begin as planned.[282]

THE CROSSING

At 7:25 p.m. on March 23, the 1st Commando Brigade began their crossing of the Rhine, and at 9:00 p.m.m XXX Corps began crossing with the Black Watch of the 51st Highland Division in the lead. Just four minutes later, Horrocks received the radio message that the Black Watch had landed safely on the far bank. After the Highlanders completed their crossing, the 15th Scottish Division crossed and landed between Wesel and Rees at 2:00 a.m. March 24. The crossing was unopposed, but later the Scotts encountered determined resistance from machine-gun nests. Meanwhile, after ferocious fighting, the Commando Brigade entered Wesel. Montgomery had established a foothold on the far side of the Rhine.[283]

The crossing of the U.S. Ninth Army was less difficult. The German forces opposite the Americans were weakened by artillery fire and aerial bombing to the point that resistance was minimal. The 30th Division led the Ninth Army, landing south of Wesel. The landing of the 79th Division followed suit

---

282 Allen, *One More River*, 212-213.; Ibid., 233.; Montgomery, *Normandy to the Baltic*, 204.
283 Allen, *One More River*, 236-242.

and was also able to land without major difficulties. American casualties were minimal. German resistance to the Scottish landings continued with some effect, as there were armored counterattacks. Nevertheless, landings on the east bank of the Rhine River continued throughout the night and morning. By the evening of March 24, the U.S. forces had already built a pontoon bridge across the river.[284]

On March 24, 1945, in conjunction with Operation Plunder, the Allies also launched Operation Varsity, which was to support the British Second Army and the U.S. Ninth Army in their mission to secure a firm foothold on the other side of the Rhine. It was carried out by the British 6th Airborne Division and U.S. 17th Airborne Division. This combined airborne force was to disrupt the German defenses north of Wesel, capture the towns of Schnappenberg and Hamminkeln, clear the Diersfordterwald of German forces, and secure three bridges over the Ijssel River.[285]

The airborne landings threw the Germans into confusion. The 17th Airborne Division quickly captured the village Diersfordt and the Diersfordterwald and secured two bridges over the Ijssel River, while the 6th Airborne Division took Hamminkeln and secured several bridges over the Ijssel River. Later that day, the 17th Airborne Division linked up with the 1st Commando Brigade at Wesel. The paratroopers of Operation Varsity secured all their objectives and took 3,500 German prisoners. Operation Varsity was a success in that it greatly facilitated the operations of the Second British and U.S. Ninth Armies that day. Also, the capture of the bridges over the Ijssel River would facilitate future 21st Army Group operations. Though often criticized as a waste of resources and lives, Operation Varsity accomplished all Montgomery wanted it to.[286]

---

284 Ibid., 247-248.
285 Montgomery, *Normandy to the Baltic*, 203.
286 Ibid., 206.

SUMMARY

The Rhine River crossing operations in 1945 demonstrated the differences between Bradley's philosophy of exploiting battlefield situations to "bounce" across the river, as the First Army did at Remagen and the Third Army did at Oppenheim, and Montgomery's philosophy that a successful crossing of the Rhine could only be done through careful planning, massive resource accumulation, and precise coordination of forces. The time Montgomery spent preparing for his crossing irritated some American commanders. Again the 21st Army Group was the main Allied effort for logistics, and Bradley's 12th Army Group had to make do with what was left over. Logistical consideration caused Eisenhower to limit the Remagen bridgehead to just five divisions, and First Army was limited to advancing just one thousand yards per day. A week after crossing at Remagen, First Army reached the Cologne-Frankfurt autobahn, an important transportation asset, but Eisenhower ordered Hodges' forces to halt until Montgomery's forces crossed the Rhine, scheduled for March 23, 1945.[287]

"Bouncing the Rhine" was effective for the Americans; however, the enemy situation opposite the area where the 21st Army Group was to cross the Rhine was much more organized and formidable than where the Americans crossed farther south. Montgomery had to devote more time and resources to his crossing operations for them to succeed; it would take a set-piece battle for the 21st Army Group to get across. This fit in well with Montgomery's philosophy, as he was a master of the set-piece battle. He intended to get a significant amount of combat power, enough for major combat operations, across in a single day. In their previous crossings at Remagen and Oppenheim, the Americans could not do this in less than several days.

---

287   Collins, *Lightening Joe*, 305.

CHAPTER XI:
COMMAND STRUCTURE

The relationship between Eisenhower and Montgomery reminds one of that between General George Washington and his second-in-command General Charles Lee during the Battle of Monmouth, in the American Revolutionary War. Lee, was vain, arrogant, and continuously critical of Washington's leadership. He felt he was more qualified than Washington to lead the Continental Army. Not satisfied with Lee's performance of duty during the battle or his attitude, Washington chose to relieve him and, at Lee's request, court-martial him. The court-martial found Lee guilty of disobeying orders, running from the enemy, and showing disrespect to his superior. Lee was, of course, an American soldier, not an ally. Eisenhower did not have this option. Had he relieved Montgomery, it would have damaged the Anglo-American Alliance. The most Eisenhower could do was refer the conflict to the Combined Chiefs of Staff, which, at one point, he was ready to do. If Montgomery had been an

American, it is entirely possible he would have been relieved.[288]

Eisenhower shared some characteristics with Montgomery. He was ambitious, a strict disciplinarian, and short-tempered as well. However, Eisenhower also could use charm to placate people. Even Montgomery felt Eisenhower's strength was in his human qualities, not in his strategic or command abilities. He readily acknowledged Eisenhower's position as the Supreme Allied Commander. However, he did not believe Eisenhower had the experience or knowledge to be both Supreme Commander and Ground Force Commander.

Montgomery knew full well, even before Operation Overlord launched, that Eisenhower would assume the position as Ground Force Commander when he determined the time was right to do so. This occurred on September 1, 1944. Montgomery's persistent disagreement with Eisenhower over strategy and command was a clear bid to retain, and later to regain, his position as Ground Force Commander.

However, not only was Eisenhower well within his rights as Supreme Allied Commander to assume the role of the ground force commander, the demographics of the Allied military environment in Europe required him to do so, or at least to appoint another American to that position. The Air Forces Commander, Air Marshal Trafford Leigh-Mallory, was British, as was the Naval Forces Commander, Admiral Bertram Ramsay, but on the ground, American resources outnumbered British and Commonwealth resources by a huge margin. Even within the British contingent, a majority of the armored vehicles were provided by the United States as well as all of the self-propelled artillery.

The number of Allied Armies was also telling. On September 16, when the 6th U.S. Army Group, commanded by General Jacob

---

288 David Wade, "Battle of Monmouth," *Military History*, (June 1998), accessed February 25, 2016, http://www.historynet.com/battle-of-monmouth.htm.

Devers, became operational, there were four American Armies in Europe, the First, Third, Seventh, and Ninth Armies. There were two British Armies, the First Canadian and the Second British Armies. The French had one, the First French Army, which belonged to Devers' 6th Army Group. With such a majority of American combat strength on the ground, it was imperative that an American serve as the ground commander.[289]

All of this meant nothing to Montgomery, who explained to Eisenhower his view that Eisenhower was too busy with his duties as the supreme commander to give the ground operations the proper attention they require. He recommended that Eisenhower appoint a deputy commander for ground operations. Montgomery felt he was the obvious choice for this position, but he stated either he or Bradley must be that man, and he would be willing to serve under Bradley. Were he appointed the ground force commander, he insisted he would still retain the direct command of the 21st Army Group.

To Eisenhower, this was unrealistic. Eisenhower paid no mind to the argument that he was too busy to coordinate the operations of three Army Groups. Anyone appointed as his deputy for ground operations would still have to deal with three Army Group Commanders, just as he was doing. The fact of the matter was that of those three, the only one causing dissension and confusion was Montgomery.[290]

Unlike Montgomery, Bradley was mild-tempered and consistently displayed an air of humility. Like Montgomery, he was demanding and not slow to relieve subordinate commanders. Also like Montgomery, he had a brilliant military mind and was loath to take chances. Therefore, while Bradley would never

---

[289] Blumenson, *Battle of the Generals*, 263.; Neillands, *The Battle for the Rhine*, 34.; Eisenhower, Crusade in Europe, 313.

[290] Butcher, *My Three Years*, 740.; Montgomery, *Memoirs*, 272; Eisenhower, *Crusade in Europe*, 284-285.

win any spectacular victories, he would also never suffer a disastrous defeat. He had the soldier's eye to see opportunities on the battlefield, but he lacked the nerve to take advantage of them. He could make instant decisions but would then agonize over them. He initiated brilliant maneuvers, only to abort them because he lacked the confidence to see them through. This is what happened on the southern wing at Falaise.[291] Bradley did not share Patton's experience and proven success as a battlefield commander. Thus, Montgomery would never look upon him as an equal.

Patton and Montgomery might have worked well together because they respected each other. The perfect team might have been Bradley as the overall ground commander with Montgomery and Patton as the two Army Group Commanders, with Patton being the most effective combat commander of the group.[292] Eisenhower, however, would never agree to this, nor would General Marshall. Patton and Montgomery had shown they could work together when both were Army Commanders in Sicily, even though both were prima donnas. When Montgomery became bogged down before Catania, Patton was allowed greater freedom to advance and divert some of the enemy opposing Montgomery. Patton's speedy advance toward Palermo impressed Montgomery, and they came to have a grudging respect for each other. While they were competitive, they were able to determine mutually acceptable solutions to challenges.[293]

Another issue was Montgomery himself. He was vastly unpopular with many U.S. and Canadian Generals, but many of his British peers also detested him. Air Marshal Tedder, the Deputy Supreme Allied Commander, and Air Chief Marshal Coningham, the 2nd Tactical Air Force commander, were just

---

291 Command Decisions, 278.
292 Ibid., 273.
293 Blumenson, *The Battle of the Generals*, 27.; Ibid., 60.

a few of them. Montgomery was detested, as British historian Robin Neillands pointed out, because he was indeed detestable. He was vain, dictatorial, obsessive, disagreeable to his peers and superiors, and not above tinkering with the truth. These are unprofessional traits, and his possession of them disqualified him from consideration as a potential ground force commander.

In spite of all of this, the lower ranking officers and enlisted men of 21st Army Group worshiped Montgomery. They knew that he would be stingy with their lives. He had to be, as British manpower still available in Britain was nearing the bottom of the barrel. Montgomery's conservation of the lives of his men originated from his experiences in the First World War. In return, Montgomery's men fought hard for him. This relationship continued throughout the war and failed only once, after Operation Goodwood. During that operation, Montgomery felt the 7th Armored, the 50th Northumbrian, and the 51st Highland Divisions did not fight as hard as they should have, and their commanders were relieved and sent home.

However, as in any Combined or Joint Force, the commander must build a team horizontally as well as vertically. Montgomery demonstrated on all occasions that he was incapable of doing this. In the latter stages of the North African Campaign, he took every opportunity to disparage General Anderson, the First Army Commander, as well as the American Commanders. In Sicily, he annoyed the Americans. In Italy, he attacked the competence of his Army Group Commander General Alexander and was slow to support General Mark Clark, the Fifth Army Commander at Salerno. Montgomery's tragedy was that, except for Alanbrooke, he never built a personal or professional relationship with his superior officers. In some cases, he never attempted to do so. The fault here rests with him. General Eisenhower showed vast amounts of tolerance toward Montgomery and was often going to his defense when the SHAEF staff attacked him. Eisenhower received neither loyalty nor gratitude in return.[294]

Despite all this, the British press and the Imperial General Staff were pushing for Montgomery to be installed as the overall ground commander, as he had been for the Normandy operation. Churchill even discussed the possibility of reinstating Montgomery as the overall ground force commander with General Marshall. Marshall replied that there would be no commander between Eisenhower and his army group commanders. He went on to say that Montgomery was not a team player. Montgomery had never gone to Eisenhower's headquarters, always forcing his superior to go to his. It was not Montgomery's eccentric behavior that angered Marshall; what he could not accept was Montgomery's open contempt for his superior officer.[295]

Also, both Generals Bradley and Patton openly stated they would resign rather than serve under Montgomery.

Montgomery's work *The Path to Leadership* (1961) contains a chapter on Churchill and Alanbrooke. Here, he wrote that "Alanbrooke was, of course, my military chief throughout the war."[296] This sentiment is inaccurate. From the time he took command of the Eighth Army in Egypt in August 1942 until he gave it up in December 1943, General Harold Alexander was his military chief, and from January 1944 until the end of the war it was General Eisenhower. This misconception by Montgomery led to many of the difficulties in his relationships with his actual commanders.

Eisenhower felt Montgomery's attitude toward the Allied command system was the most difficult business he had to handle in the war. In a message to Montgomery on October 13, a frustrated Eisenhower wrote, "The real issue at hand is

---

294 Neillands, *The Battle for the Rhine*, 37-44.; Delaforce, *Monty's Highlanders*, 141.
295 Pogue, *George C. Marshall*, 510-517.
296 Montgomery, *The Path to Leadership*, 122.

not command, it is Antwerp. Your plan that involves further movement toward the Rhine must be postponed until the capture of the approaches to Antwerp can be assured. I keep reverting again and again to the matter of getting Antwerp into a workable condition. The Combined Chiefs of Staff are considering giving me a direct order to ensure the capture of the approaches to Antwerp takes precedence over all other operations. I do not agree that one man can stay so close to the day to day movement of divisions and corps that he can keep a battle grip upon the overall situation and direct it intelligently. This is no longer a Normandy beachhead! My present plan is based upon the conviction that 21st Army Group, with its commitments in Antwerp, and thereafter for thrusting into the northern sections of Holland, will be left with such depleted forces facing eastwards that it could be expected to do nothing more than to carry out strong flanking operations supporting the main attack upon the Ruhr. For this reason, the plan calls for assigning the capture of the Ruhr to 12th Army Group with 21st Army Group operating in a supporting role in the north."[297]

Montgomery replied three days later that Eisenhower would hear no more on the subject of command and signed the message "Your very devoted and loyal subordinate."[298]

Here Eisenhower addressed not only the command framework but Montgomery's criticism, often outside the chain of command, of Eisenhower's broad-front policy. Montgomery believed Eisenhower should adopt a narrow-front strategy and attack north of the Ruhr, through northern Germany, and on to Berlin. At first, Montgomery envisioned a force of forty divisions, which would need fear for nothing, commanded by him to execute this campaign. Later, he revised the force

---

[297] Chandler, ed, *The Papers of Dwight David Eisenhower*, 2220-2223.
[298] Pogue, *George C. Marshall*, 511.

structure to the First Canadian Army, the 2nd British Army, and the First American Army of twelve divisions, all under his command.[299] This would leave the 12th Army Group with just the Third Army, and the Ninth Army. It would also mean diverting 12th Army Group's logistical resources to Montgomery and placing the Third Army in a defense. Montgomery was referring to his discussions on the topic with Eisenhower when he wrote, "In August 1944, I urged we must finish the war this year, the Germans were on their last legs. But I was unable to persuade the Americans to take the risk which, in any case, was nil. So it was not done, and the war went into 1945 thus increasing our post-war political problems, and tragically wasting a great many valuable young lives."[300]

Montgomery wanted to be the Allied commander who took Berlin. He saw his single-thrust concept as the only way he could accomplish the capture of that city. However, Eisenhower's mission in Europe, from the point of view of the Combined Chiefs of Staff, was the destruction of Germany's Armed Forces. As such, the destruction of the enemy forces was always the guiding principle of Allied operations. Therefore, Eisenhower was more concerned with the defeat of the German Army and the SS than he was with the capture of Berlin, not to mention the untold casualties that would most certainly be the result of an assault on Berlin.[301]

Montgomery's Chief of Staff later wrote, "Even if we had been able to get a sizable force across the Rhine in the autumn, the Germans would have produced sufficient troops to strangle its effectiveness. The flanks of our salient would have been particularly vulnerable. In my opinion, Eisenhower was right when he decided he could not concentrate sufficient resources to

---

299   Montgomery, *Memoirs*, 241-242.
300   Montgomery, *Normandy to the Baltic*, 120.
301   Eisenhower, *Crusade in Europe*, 225-226.

allow one strong thrust deep into Germany north of the Rhine, with any hope of success. If he had halted Patton, and diverted all of his resources to 21st Army Group, I think it is possible we could have gotten a bridgehead over the Rhine before winter, but not more. I need not belittle Montgomery nor deny him any of his luster to rate Eisenhower his superior as a field commander."[302]

During the Battle of the Bulge, the British press once again began campaigning for Montgomery to be appointed as the overall ground commander. General Marshall was aware of this press campaign. He telephoned Eisenhower and told him, "Under no circumstances make any concessions of any kind whatsoever." When Montgomery renewed his criticisms of the command arrangements, stating it was, in fact, the existing command system that had led to the battle, Eisenhower had had enough and decided to ask the Combined Chiefs of Staff to choose between him and Montgomery. de Guingand intervened and convinced Eisenhower not to involve the Combined Chiefs of Staff.[303]

---

[302] De Guingand, *Operation Victory*, 412-413.
[303] Eisenhower, *Crusade in Europe*, 356.; Pogue, *George C. Marshall*, 511. De Guingand, *Operation Victory*, 434-435.

CHAPTER XII:
CONCLUSION

During the Battles of Alam Halfa, August-September 1942, and Second Alamein, October-November 1942, Montgomery displayed initiative, daring, and flexibility that led to victory in both instances. Second Alamein brought Montgomery fame, celebrity, and the reputation as the Allies' most professional and competent commander. After all, it was the first Allied victory of the war that sent German forces into a full-scale retreat. However, those characteristics of generalship that Montgomery displayed in the late summer and autumn of 1942 would not be seen again until September 1944, with disastrous results at Arnhem. After the death of his wife Betty in 1937, Montgomery dedicated his life to the Army, at the expense of his relationships with his two sons. The defeat of Rommel at Second Alamein placed Montgomery at the top of his profession, not in rank or duty position, but in fame and admiration. With his new standing in the Army came a determination to preserve that reputation and celebrity.[304]

Montgomery's pursuit of Rommel across Libya is more accurately described as his *following* of Rommel across Libya. There was no significant contact between the British Eighth Army and Panzer Army Africa between Second Alamein and the Battle of the Mareth Line, four months after Rommel's withdrawal from Alamein. How many lives were lost and resources expended during those months? If Montgomery had destroyed Panzer Army Africa in November 1942, as he possessed great enough superiority in men and material to do, the Allied campaign in North Africa would have been concluded months before it was. With control of the Mediterranean, the Allies could have transported the victorious Eighth Army to Tripoli or even to Sfax in Tunisia. There, the Eighth could have assisted against the German Fifth Panzer Army. The Allies could have closed out the North African Campaign in January or February 1943, instead of May 1943.

In Sicily, Montgomery's opposition to the original invasion plan was based on protecting his reputation and feeding his ego. It centered on the proposed landing of the U.S. Seventh Army in the vicinity of Palermo. If this happened, there would be no one to protect Montgomery's left flank. Also, a landing near Palermo would give Patton direct access to the northern coastal road leading to Messina, before the Germans and Italians coud emplace defensive positions in the mountains west and southwest of Messina. Therefore, Montgomery complained and bullied until his superiors changed the plan and landed the Seventh Army on his left, in a secondary role. Montgomery was content as he did not have to worry about an open flank. Then, when he had difficulties breaking through the Catania Plain, he pushed the Americans out of his way and seized Highway

---

304   Montgomery, *Memoirs*, 41.

124 to get around Mount Etna. Now the Americans had no roads to Messina. The original invasion plan had more potential for getting Allied Forces to Messina more quickly. Montgomery did what he had to do to get his plan adopted, it took too long to get to Messina, and too many Germans and Italians, along with their equipment, were able to escape.

The greatest harm Montgomery's generalship did to an Allied campaign concerns the failure to open the Port of Antwerp quickly and cross the Lower Rhine. Both of these operations were huge, complex, and planned and executed concurrently. A few factors led to their failure. First, the First Canadian Army, charged with clearing the Scheldt Estuary, was exhausted from its successful pursuit of the Germans after crossing the Seine River. Second, Montgomery chose not to allocate sufficient forces from the British Second Army to assist in opening the Estuary. Finally, Montgomery did not provide enough equal command emphasis to the simultaneous planning and execution of two major operations, what is now referred to as multitasking.

In fairness, it is highly probable that no other commander could have done what Montgomery endeavored to do. However, the Allies had to get the Port of Antwerp opened as soon as possible, if it was to be any of any use to Allied Operations beyond the Rhine and if the war in the west was to be won in 1944. Military expediency and common sense dictated that Antwerp must be opened before operations across the Rhine could be executed. Montgomery was then concerned with the criticism he received for the delay in taking Caen and, unjustly, for the failure to close the Falaise gap. Justified or not, Montgomery felt the criticism tarnished his reputation, and he needed to do something spectacular to restore his luster. Getting his army group over the Rhine River before Bradley would, Montgomery felt, make people forget about Caen and Falaise.

Getting across the Rhine consumed Montgomery. Even before his troops took Antwerp, he received permission from Eisenhower to plan Operation Market Garden, and he was immersed in that planning during operations in Antwerp. So was his subordinate commander. This misplaced focus led to the most catastrophic mistake of the war. After capturing Antwerp on September 4, Montgomery's forces neglected to pursue elements of the German Fifteenth Army north of Antwerp and failed to prevent their occupation of the Scheldt Estuary. The German presence in the Scheldt denied the Allies the use of until the end of November.

Had the Allies had Antwerp as a viable port in mid-to-late September 1944, their logistical problems would have been solved. The drives of the American First and Third Armies, which slowed in September because of a change in priority of logistical support to Montgomery for Market Garden, could have resumed sooner. Perhaps then the bloody fighting in the Hurtgen Forest could have been avoided. With sufficient logistical support, which Antwerp would have provided, the Allies could have closed on the Rhine before the end of 1944 and the Germans would not have had the opportunity to launch their Ardennes Offensive, known to the Allies as the Battle of the Bulge. The effect of Montgomery's generalship, influenced by his selfishness and egotism, in September 1944 was just that significant.

Because of the failure to open Antwerp, doubts persisted about Montgomery's combat flexibility and ability to take advantage of opportunities as they presented themselves. While it was true he had defeated the undersupplied and equipped Rommel at Alam Halfa and Second Alamein, he had never commanded a successful envelopment. Nowhere since Second Alamein had Montgomery demonstrated a combat prowess that deserved any undue praise. Montgomery's armies had fought workmanlike campaigns in North Africa, Sicily, Italy, and France, but in none of these did they demonstrate the initiative, daring, or flexibility of the Germans or Americans.[305]

There are three tenets of British military professionalism; approach, study, and followership. Study is being well read and versed in the profession of arms. As Montgomery was both, there is no need to question this aspect of his professionalism. However, Montgomery did show deficiencies in the areas of approach—how one relates to others, specifically peers and subordinates—and followership—loyalty to your leaders and obeying not only their orders but their intent.[306]

Montgomery tended to show his peers or near peers little respect or consideration. Of his group, Patton and Bradley come off pretty well in Montgomery's writings. He always treated them with consideration when he interacted with them. However, he treated Generals Anderson of the First British Army, and Auchinleck of the Eighth Army in North Africa with complete disrespect and disdain. Perhaps because he knew he would one day be compared to them? He tried to assassinate their characters through his messages to Alanbrooke and Alexander. He held his peers in the Royal Air Force in contempt as well, especially Air Marshal Tedder, Eisenhower's Deputy Commander in Europe.

Montgomery's deficiencies in the area of followership were, without a doubt, the most important aspect of his professionalism. Except for Field Marshal Alanbrooke and Alexander in North Africa, Montgomery could not get along with any of his commanders. He was disloyal and insubordinate to Auchinleck in the Southeast Command and in Egypt. Although he had no complaints about Alexander in North Africa, this changed in Sicily. Once he began to have difficulties on the Catania Plain, he wrote to Alanbrooke and even to Commanders in other theaters

---

305   Hastings, *Armageddon*, 26-27.
306   "Sandhurst Guide to Developing Leaders," *SO2 Leadership* (Camberley UK.: Royal Military Academy Sandhurst, 2012), 28-29.

of operations about Alexander's deficiencies as an Army Group Commander. This attitude persisted in Italy and continued until Montgomery returned to England in January 1944.

The greatest displays of disloyalty and insubordination, Montgomery reserved for Eisenhower. Montgomery was consistently critical of Eisenhower, who was his Supreme Commander in North Africa, beginning with Operation Torch, through Sicily, Italy, and finally in Europe. Montgomery believed Eisenhower was inexperienced, had no grasp of strategy, and was not a battlefield commander. Though entitled to his opinion, as a professional officer, Montgomery should have kept his opinions to himself, as officers are often required to do. Instead, he took every opportunity to disparage Eisenhower, and General Marshall, to Churchill and Alanbrooke. Not only was Montgomery disloyal, he was also insubordinate and disrespectful to Eisenhower on several occasions during their meetings. Knowing full well Eisenhower's intent of opening the Scheldt Estuary, he finally convinced Eisenhower to let him defer that operation until after Market Garden, with grave consequences for the Allied war effort in Europe.

Eisenhower, whose professionalism was above reproach, wrote *Eisenhower's Own Story of the War: The Complete Report of the Supreme Commander on the War in Europe From the Day of Invasion to the Day of Victory* (1946). This work contains not a single negative word about Montgomery. Eisenhower went out of his way to avoid controversial issues. Regarding the chain of command, about which Montgomery gave Eisenhower much trouble and stress, Eisenhower wrote, "In the matter of command, it can be said here that all relationships between American and British forces were smooth and effective."[307] He avoids any

---

[307] Dwight Eisenhower, *Eisenhower's Own Story of the War: The Complete Report of the Supreme Commander on the War in Europe From the Day of Invasion to the Day of Victory* (New York: ARCO Publishing, 1946), 35-37.

criticism of Montgomery for his delays in taking Caen, even following Montgomery's party line that the immediate seizure of Caen had never been part of the plan but operations in the vicinity of Caen would draw the German Armor to Caen making it easier for the Americans to break out in the West. He also leaves out any reference to Montgomery's failure to clear the approaches to the Port of Antwerp to facilitate the Allied attack into Germany. Eisenhower does mention that even though Operation Market Garden failed to force a crossing of the Lower Rhine River at Arnhem, the operation did provide "very positive and important advantages to our forces."[308] Eisenhower does not say what those positive and important advantages were.

Montgomery did have serious professional shortcomings and, on occasion, showed surprising lapses in judgment and behavior. His inability to get along with his military colleagues is well documented and reached catastrophic proportions in his relations with Eisenhower. He also allowed his desire for personal glory to influence his planning. These are the words of Dr. Norman Dixon, a psychologist who served in the British Army during the war. He believes Montgomery was naturally cautious and meticulous. However, his quest for glory and attention overpowered his natural characteristics. This is why Montgomery was in such a hurry to carry out Operation Market Garden, for it promised to gratify his wish to win the race to Berlin. His persistence about Market Garden was more than just a quest for glory; it was also a result of his fear of failure. He had to be looked upon as the most competent and successful commander on either side in the war; if not, his narcissism would have made him feel a failure, even if he had won every battle he fought. This is why Montgomery always took the credit for the successes of his subordinates and others.[309]

---

308   Ibid., 38-40.
309   Dixon, *On the Psychology*, 359.; Ibid., 145.

Field Marshal Alexander later wrote, "Montgomery was unwise to always take the credit for battlefield successes for himself. His prestige would have been even higher if he had given some credit to those responsible for his victories."[310] Montgomery developed a quasi-paranoid streak of self-justification, a noxious insistence that all his battles and campaigns had gone exactly according to plan. These claims were so obviously untrue that some historians saw him as a boastful and suspect figure. Boastful and suspect he may have been, as well as unprofessional, but he was an effective, determined, and competent, though not "great" general.[311]

The six core values of the British Army relate very closely to military professionalism. They are selfless commitment, courage, discipline, integrity, loyalty, and respect for others. Montgomery's courage and discipline are beyond question. Indeed, he could serve as a role model for these two core values. However, he had severe deficiencies in the remaining four.

While Montgomery was selflessly committed to the British Army as an institution, the core value of selfless commitment refers to more than that. It also relates to the mission and the men. He put himself before the mission at Alam Halfa and Second Alamein, where it required aggressive pursuit and destruction of Rommel's forces. Not wanting to risk diminishing his victory at Alam Halfa, he did not pursue; not wanting to risk a setback after Second Alamein, he decided not to pursue aggressively. Both courses of action were counter to the orders Alexander had issued to him for Alamein, which Montgomery himself wrote were quite simple: destroy Rommel and his Army. The most glaring example of this was Montgomery's failure to clear the Scheldt Estuary and open the Port of Antwerp in September 1944 because he was anxious to execute Operation

---

310   Alexander, *Memoirs*, 16.
311   Hamilton, *Monty: The Making of a General*, 606.

Market Garden. He placed his desire to be first across the Rhine River over the needs of the Allied coalition.[312]

Montgomery's integrity was often called into question. The falsehoods he spread concerning General Auchinleck and the withdrawal order is an example. Patton and Bradley certainly questioned Montgomery's integrity in Sicily after Montgomery cut off Bradley's II Corps and "stole" Highway 124, without any prior coordination with the Americans, or authorization by Alexander. His false report to Alanbrooke, not to mention his false press release during Operation Goodwood, as well as his insistence that his operations always went according to his plans, when they obviously did not, as Catania, Caen, Antwerp, and Arnhem show, were all products of a man who was loose with his integrity.

Perhaps the most unprofessional examples of Montgomery's lack of integrity were the orders from his superiors he ignored when they did not suit him. General Eisenhower remembered asking Montgomery if he ever followed orders after he had ignored orders from SHAEF (Supreme Headquarters Allied Expeditionary Force). Montgomery replied that if he did not like the orders, he would go as far as he could in disobedience and try to bluff his way through. At least he was being honest in describing his lack of integrity.[313]

Montgomery displayed an unprofessional lack of loyalty to his superiors throughout the war, which we have already reviewed in detail. Suffice it to say that he was so deficient in this core value that De Guingand wrote, "Though Montgomery demanded absolute loyalty to himself and hated intriguers, he often displayed lack of loyalty to his superiors, and was himself an intriguer, a habit that almost cost him his command at the

---

[312] P. J. McCormack, "Leadership: Proceedings of a Symposium Held at the Royal Military Academy Sandhurst." *Sandhurst Occasional Papers no. 18*, (Camberley, UK: Royal Military Academy Sandhurst, 2014). 22-24.; Montgomery, *Memoirs*, 93.
[313] Alexander, *Memoirs*, 16.

end of 1944 when Eisenhower lost patience with him."[314]

This comment by De Guingand also condemns Montgomery under the sixth core value, respect for others. Montgomery's disloyalty and intriguing against others revealed his disrespect for others.

Montgomery's greatest contribution to Allied victory in the Second World War was in modifying the Overlord plan, not Second Alamein. If Auchinleck had remained in command of the Eighth Army with the material advantages enjoyed by Montgomery, there might not have been a Second Alamein as Auchinleck probably would have counterattacked and destroyed Rommel and his army after Alam Halfa.

However, the Allies were not going to defeat Germany until they crossed the channel and invaded Fortress Europe. Operation Overlord was the key event leading to the defeat of Germany in the west, and whether one admires Montgomery or not, he was the key to the success of Overlord. Patton might have been too aggressive on Normandy and sustained too many casualties, Alexander might have been too timid about the weather and recommended delaying the invasion, but Montgomery did everything right on June 6, 1944, regardless of whether he took Caen that day. All free peoples owe a debt to Field Marshal Bernard Law Montgomery, 1st Viscount of Alamein, for that. Nigel Hamilton wrote, "His legacy to the Allied Armies endures today: training, and rehearsal, and professionalism in the handling of men and women . . . and care among commanders to preserve human life . . . Arrogant, vain, boastful, boorish, and bigoted, he wanted to win . . . Lacking magnanimity, he went to his grave embattled, lonely and haunted."[315]

---

314 De Guingand, *From Brass Hat*, 14
315 Nigel Hamilton, *Monty The Battles of Field Marshal Bernard Montgomery* (New York: Random House, 1994), preface.

APPENDIX 1:
THE LITERATURE

The most important decision concerning the prosecution of the war to come out of Anglo-American cooperation was the "Germany first" strategy; however, the British and the Americans had different operational theories about accomplishing this strategy. The Americans believed the best way to assist the Russians and to strike a decisive blow against Germany was an invasion of France. The British felt the "soft underbelly" of Europe, the Mediterranean area, was the best way to break into Europe and strike at Germany. Yet to perform operations, they had to cooperate.[316] Field Marshal Montgomery would sorely test this cooperation.

In the spring of 1942, Britain had been at war for two and a half years and other than the Royal Air Force's victory in the Battle of Britain in 1940 and some minor successes in Africa

---

316 Bernard Wasserstein, *Barbarism and Civilization: A History of Europe In Our Time* (Oxford: Oxford University Press, 2007), 327.

against the Italians in 1940 and 1941, there was little cause for jubilation. All of Britain's endeavors in the war seemed to be failing. British forces, defeated alongside the French in northern Europe in 1940, were being pushed back toward India in Asia. An expedition to Norway had failed, as did one to the Balkans. In May of 1941, the British Army surrendered Crete. After suffering all of these failures, there was yet one more the British would have to endure, the disaster of the Dieppe Raid, Operation Jubilee in August 1942.

The British South Eastern Command commander, Lieutenant General Bernard Law Montgomery, planned this operation. Although he was sent to Egypt before it executed in August 1942, Terence Robertson explained in *Dieppe: The Shame and the Glory* (1962) that Montgomery developed the plan which contributed to the raid's failure. Montgomery attempted to explain this away in his *Memoirs* (1958).

Montgomery's involvement in the Dieppe raid would show the beginning of two trends that would mark Montgomery's career in World War Two: the changing of an initial plan that he could not call his own and explaining away any failure that involved him. However, the lessons he learned from the Dieppe raid would serve him well in Operation Overlord.

On August 13, 1942, Montgomery usurped command of the British Eighth Army in Egypt from General Claude Auchinleck two days before he officially assumed command. Nigel Hamilton, in his *Master of the Battlefield: Monty's War Years 1942-1944* (1983), provided a very detailed chronology of the actions Montgomery took in Egypt before assuming command of the Eighth Army, actions he was not authorized to take. In July 1942, General Auchinleck had defeated Rommel in the First Battle of Alamein.

The First Battle of Alamein was superbly explained by

Jonathan Dimbleby in *Destiny in the Desert: The Road to Alamein—The Battle that Turned the Tide of World War II* (2013). Not only was General Auchinleck's generalship in the battle detailed, so was Rommel's reaction to his defeat and his praise of Auchinleck. Another historian who has contributed to the literature of the First Battle of Alamein is Philip Warner. The chapter he wrote, "Auchinleck," in *Churchill's Generals* (1991), edited by John Keegan, exposed some of Montgomery's questionable statements and actions to discredit Auchinleck, his predecessor in command. The events Warner cited also appeared in Montgomery's memoirs and Nigel Hamilton's works.

Both Montgomery's memoirs and his *El Alamein to the River Sangro* (1958) provide much information on Montgomery's preparations for his first encounter with Rommel in North Africa, the Battle of Alam Halfa in August 1942. John Keegan's *The Second World War* (1989) is an excellent general history of the war, and the text devoted to Alam Halfa is interesting. Keegan suggested that Montgomery recognized that he lacked the skills to "out-Rommel" Rommel. He also pointed out that Auchinleck had destroyed much of Panzer Army Africa's offensive power in the First Battle of Alamein, and, as a result, Panzer Army Africa lacked any substantial offensive capability even before Montgomery even arrived in Egypt.[317] Montgomery's defensive success at Alam Halfa was his first victory in the Second World War.

Montgomery's most famous victory and the one that established his reputation was the Battle of Second Alamein in October to November 1942. Montgomery's memoirs, as well as the memoirs by General Brian Horrocks, *A Full Life* (1960), provide information concerning Montgomery's command of the battle, and F.W. Winterbotham's *The Ultra Secret* (1974) offers

---

317   John Keegan, *The Second World War* (London: Penguin Books, 1989), 336.

thoughtful insight into how Ultra affected its outcome.

The Memoirs of Field Marshal Kesselring (2007) provides some insight into how the German command viewed Montgomery's generalship. Kesselring, commander of Axis forces in the Mediterranean area, believed Montgomery strove for safety and was correspondingly methodical. Rommel always knew Montgomery would allow time for him to break contact, withdraw, and maintain his orderly and efficient retreat.[318] Friedrich Ruge's *Rommel in Normandy* (1979) adds to this impression of Montgomery being overly cautious. After Rommel's defeat at Second Alamein, Churchill, General Alexander, then commander of Middle East Command, and Air Marshal John Tedder, Commander of RAF Middle East, all urged Montgomery to pursue Panzer Army Africa. Francis De Guingand explained in *Generals at War* (1964) that Montgomery refused to initiate a pursuit until he tidied up the battlefield, even though De Guingand had already assembled the required transportation and supplies.[319] The British Eighth Army never did destroy their German and Italian adversaries. After seven months of pursuit, Panzer Group Africa surrendered to the British First Army. The history of the pursuit has been chronicled in great detail in *The Destruction of the Axis Forces in Africa* (2009) by I.S.O. Playfair.

Carlo D'Este's *Bitter Victory: The Battle for Sicily, 1943* (2008) and B.H. Liddell Hart's *History of the Second World War* (1970) are excellent sources of detailed information on overall operations in Sicily. The plan for the invasion of Sicily labeled Operation Husky called for Patton's American Seventh Army and Montgomery's Eighth Army to land in a staggered fashion over a four-day period, and then to cut off and defeat the German army there. Hanson Baldwin explained in *Battles*

---

[318] Albert Kesselring, *The Memoirs of Field Marshal Kesselring* (London: Greenhill Books, 2007), 140.
[319] Francis De Guingand, *Generals at War* (London: Hodder and Stoughton, 1964), 68.

Lost and Won: Great Campaigns of World War II (1966) that Montgomery once again widely condemned an initial plan as inviting disaster. And yet again, Montgomery had a plan for the taking of Sicily. Even though the American Army and Corps commanders preferred the initial plan, as did the British Naval Commander-in-Chief, Admiral of the Fleet Sir Andrew Cunningham, Montgomery had his way. Eisenhower approved Montgomery's version of Operation Husky on May 13, 1943, just two months before it was to commence.[320] His plan was unsuccessful, for as Bernard Wasserstein pointed out in *Barbarism and Civilization: A History of Europe In Our Time* (2007), over 100,000 Italian and German Troops and most of their equipment escaped to Italy. Forrest Pogue, in his *George C. Marshall: Organizer of Victory 1943-1945* (1973) explained how General George C. Marshall was impressed by neither Montgomery nor his plan and was concerned that Montgomery's arrogant unwillingness to consider other points of view would lead to untold errors.[321]

After Sicily, the British Eighth Army under Montgomery invaded Italy. For overall operations in Italy, this work makes use of John Strawson's *The Italian Campaign* (1987), and Albert Garland and Howard Smyth's *Sicily and the Surrender of Italy* (1965). These histories provide the information concerning historical events which relate to Montgomery's generalship during that campaign, such as the Eighth Army's mission to reinforce the Fifth U.S. Army at Salerno. General Mark Clark's *Calculated Risk* (2007) provides his version of this operation as the Fifth Army commander. General Harold Alexander, Montgomery's commander while in Italy, gave his perspective

---

320   Hanson Baldwin, *Battles Lost and Won: Great Campaigns of World War II.* (Old Saybrook, CT.: Konecky and Konecky, 1966), 195.
321   Forrest Pogue, *George C. Marshall, Organizer of Victory 1943-1945* (New York: Viking Press, 1973), 218.

of Montgomery's march to Salerno in *Memoirs 1940-1945* (1962). The Germans deployed a small force that used natural and artificial obstacles to delay Montgomery's already slow and very cautious pursuit. This rearguard was so effective that the Eighth Army posed no serious threat to the Germans at Salerno; in fact, the issue of Salerno was decided before the Eighth Army arrived.[322]

On December 31, 1943, Montgomery left Italy and his beloved Eighth Army to assume command of the 21st Army Group and to prepare for the Allied Landings in France scheduled for May 1944. The campaign in northern Europe against Germany would last less than a year, and it would prove to be the catalyst for personal and professional conflicts between Montgomery and the Supreme Allied Commander, General Eisenhower. These conflicts would threaten the Allied unity of command, degrade Allied operations, and prolong the war in Europe. In all cases, even historians with "pro-Montgomery" tendencies agree it was Montgomery himself who initiated these conflicts, though perhaps not intentionally.

As was his usual procedure, Montgomery immediately repudiated the initial plan and insisted he be allowed to develop his own plan for the Landings at Normandy. In this case, it was fortunate that he did. He doubled the size of the landing force, significantly lengthened of the beachhead, and included the use of airborne forces to secure its flanks. All of these changes were critical to the success of the landings and Montgomery has been correctly credited with the success of the Operation Overlord. Montgomery's memoirs, General De Guingand's *Operation Victory* (1947), and General Eisenhower's *Crusade in Europe* (1948) provide valuable information on operations in Normandy.

---

[322] Kesselring, *Memoirs*, 186.

The Anglo-American goodwill that resulted from the successful landings was immediately put under strain by the British failure to take Caen on D-Day. As Richard Lamb's *Montgomery in Europe 1943-1945: Success or Failure?* (1984) pointed out, Montgomery had repeatedly declared Caen a D-Day objective. As the days went on, it became apparent that the Germans were doing their best to hold on to Caen to use as a hinge for any retreat from Normandy they might have to execute.[323] As weeks passed, Eisenhower began putting pressure on Montgomery to act more offensively in the Caen area. Repeated failures to capture the city were described in great detail in Patrick De Laforce's *Monty's Highlanders* (2000), and Lloyd Clark's *Operation Epsom* (2004). The Germans were able to delay Montgomery for almost five weeks as his armored frontal assaults were repeatedly halted before Caen. Montgomery would eventually take Caen, but at a significant loss in men, tanks, and something he could not replenish, time.[324]

Carlo D'Este in *Decision in Normandy* (1994) explained General Omar Bradley's American First Army breakout attempt, known as Operation Cobra, was to begin with the saturation bombing of the zone to his front, immediately followed by the ground attack to penetrate and exploit the gap blasted in the German defenses. Adolf Hitler ordered a counterattack along the boundary between the American and British forces in the direction of Mortain. When the German offensive failed, it appeared that General George Patton's U.S. Third Army could sweep around the German left flank and encircle the enemy. Montgomery agreed to send the First Canadian Army south to complete the encirclement of the Germans at Falaise. However, even though he blamed Montgomery for the failure to close

---

323   David Mason, *Breakout: Drive to the Seine* (New York: Ballantine Books, 1972), 106.
324   Friedrich Ruge, *Rommel in Normandy* (San Rafael, CA.: Presidio Press, 1979), 215

the gap, Omar Bradley, in *A General's Life* (1983) identified his decision to stop Patton at Argentan as the reason. Tens of thousands of Germans escaped destruction, just as happened in Sicily. Ken Tout explained the fight toward Falaise in great detail in *A Fine Night for Tanks: The Road to Falaise* (2002). The American contribution to this failure was outlined in Martin Blumensen's "General Bradley's Decision at Argentan," *Command Decisions* (1959).

Perhaps the biggest historical controversy of the war was Montgomery's failure to cross the Albert Canal and prevent the German Fifteenth Army from moving into the Scheldt from where they would deny the use of the Port of Antwerp. There were several reasons for this. The First Canadian Army was fatigued after the pursuit from the Seine. The XXX Corps Commander, General Brian Horrocks, was distracted by Montgomery's emphasis on the Rhine. And Montgomery was more concerned with the planning of Operation Market Garden.

Montgomery took Antwerp on September 4, 1944; however, it was not until the end of November 1944 that the first Allied ship entered the port. In *A Full Life* (1960), Horrocks gallantly took the blame, admitting his attention was focused on the Rhine because that is where Montgomery's focus was. He had captured the port, but securing the approaches so the port could be used never crossed his mind. Peter Beale in *The Great Mistake: The Battle for Antwerp and the Breveland Peninsula, September 1944* (2004) and Mark Zuehlke in *Terrible Victory: First Canadian Army and the Scheldt Estuary Campaign* (2007) expertly explained the results of this miscalculation. If Montgomery had secured the Scheldt Estuary, immediately upon the capture of Antwerp, perhaps the Allied logistical problems in Europe would have been solved in September or October 1944. The advance of Bradley's 12th Army Group, instead of being stopped by lack of fuel and priority, could have continued and closed on the Rhine. This would have eliminated the staging and assembly areas used by the Germans for their Ardennes Offensive that December. In such a case, the last-gasp German offensive in the west would have taken place somewhere east of the Rhine, if at all.

Montgomery was a believer in very detailed planning, and he was never concerned with how long it took for him to plan an operation. The war, he felt, would wait on him. Montgomery favored textbook attacks with enormous artillery support, he believed in what he called "walking the course," and he saw to it that every division under his command carried out meticulous preparations for their tasks in any forthcoming engagement with the enemy.[325]

Operation Market Garden was therefore outside his norm. From his conception of the operation until execution was only twenty-three days. Montgomery did not do business this way. So why did he allow himself to deviate from his usual practice? Perhaps it was his desire to be first across the Rhine, to add some luster so a reputation that lost some shine as a result of the failure to take Caen, close the Falaise Gap, and most importantly get the Port of Antwerp operational. Indeed, the execution of Operation Market Garden would only further delay the opening of Antwerp. Montgomery's focus on crossing the Rhine would cause him to fail to commit the vital forces to clear the Scheldt Estuary quickly.

Operation Market Garden, though it would liberate substantial portions of the Netherlands, would fail to force a crossing of the Rhine: there would be no exploitation of the bridgehead, no advance to establish a northern flank on the Zuider Zee nor an eastern flank on the Ijssel River. The

---

325   Patrick Delaforce, *Monty's Highlanders* (London: Chancellor Press, 2000), 36-38.

failure of Operation Market Garden cost the Allies seventeen thousand dead, wounded, or missing in nine days of heavy fighting.[326] Steven Semmes's "Decision Making in Alliance Warfare: Operation Market Garden—A Case Study" (2001) outlines the mistakes made in the abbreviated planning for the operation. Russell Weigley points out the failure to heed the human intelligence that was coming out of the objective area in *Eisenhower's Lieutenants: The Campaign of France and Germany 1944-1945* (1981).

The beginning of the German Ardennes Offensive on December 16, 1944, caught the Allies by surprise, and American unpreparedness soon became obvious. More than 200,000 Germans and almost 1,000 tanks launched in Germany's last attempt to halt the Allied advances in the West. Hitler intended to capture Antwerp by splitting the American and British armies through an attack in the Ardennes Forest, just as the Germans had done in 1940. However, this was not 1940. Eisenhower immediately reinforced the shoulders of the German penetration, and within a few days, General Patton had turned his Third U.S. Army northwards and was counterattacking against the German left flank. The battle was characterized by individual and isolated units fighting desperate actions against the Germans. Not the most critical part of the fighting but certainly the most famous was the siege of Bastogne, a transportation hub, which held out until relieved by elements of Patton's Third Army. What turned out to be one of the most controversial aspects of the battle was Eisenhower's decision to give Montgomery command of the Ninth and First U.S. Armies in the northern part of the salient, leaving Bradley's 12th Army Group with just one army, Patton's Third. This decision would result in Montgomery giving a press conference toward the end of the battle in which the Americans

---

326 Wasserstein, *Barbarism and Civilization*, 385.

felt he tried to claim the credit for turning an American defeat into a Montgomery victory. *The Bitter Woods* (1969) by John S.D. Eisenhower and *Battle: The Story of the Bulge* (1959) by John Toland were critical to the research of this battle.

On March 23, 1945, Montgomery finally realized a long-cherished goal of crossing the Rhine. The First French Army and the U.S. Seventh Army, of the 6th Army Group, were the first to reach the Rhine in November 1944, but Eisenhower ordered them not to cross. The crossing by the U.S. First Army, on March 7, 1945, was not an assault crossing, as an existing bridge was used, so Montgomery was sure he was conducting the first assault crossing of the Rhine. Unfortunately for Montgomery, and unknown to him at the time, General Patton's U.S. Third Army had executed the first assault crossing of the Rhine the night before on March 22. Montgomery's crossing of the Rhine was in size and scope second only to Normandy. Montgomery's memoirs, as well as his Normandy to the Baltic (1946), provide excellent information on his crossing of the Rhine, as does Peter Allen's *One More River: The Rhine Crossings of 1945* (1980).

Montgomery's relations with his superiors were disastrous. The only superior with which he had a good working relationship was Field Marshal Alan Brooke, also known as Lord Alanbrooke, the Chief of the Imperial General Staff. Alanbrooke's *War Diaries, 1939-1945* (2001) reveal that he repeatedly warned Montgomery about his attitude and implored him to take every measure to improve his relations with the Americans, especially Eisenhower. Alanbrooke was the only person from whom Montgomery would take advice but even he could not sway him on this particular subject,. The main cause of tension between Montgomery and the Americans was the ground command structure. Montgomery did not feel Eisenhower was militarily intelligent enough to be both the Supreme Allied Commander and the Ground Commander.

Montgomery repeatedly tried to convince Eisenhower to appoint a Ground Commander. Naturally, Montgomery felt he was the only person qualified for that position. He soon had Churchill and the British press on his side. Matters came to a head when Montgomery, in a letter to Eisenhower, blamed the Ardennes Offensive on the lack of a Ground Commander and by inference on Eisenhower. Eisenhower decided either he or Montgomery had to go. General Bedell Smith, Eisenhower's Chief of Staff, discussed the issue with Montgomery's Chief of Staff, General De Guingand. De Guingand returned to Montgomery's headquarters and briefed him. Montgomery, utterly surprised by Eisenhower's reaction, wrote a letter of apology, which Eisenhower accepted. Montgomery's retention of his command was a close-run thing and documented by De Guingand in *Generals at War* (1964) and *Operation Victory* (1947).

Other sources critical to this work are *Montgomery and the Eighth Army, A Selection from the Diaries: Correspondence and other Papers of Field Marshal The Viscount Montgomery of Alamein, August 1942 to December 1943* (1991) edited by Stephen Brooks and *The Papers of Dwight David Eisenhower. Vol. 4: The War Years* (1970), edited by Alfred Chandler. The first provides critical information in correspondence between Montgomery and other senior leaders in the British military, and the second contains Eisenhower's correspondence with Montgomery and also with General George C. Marshall.

APPENDIX 2: SIGNIFICANT DATES

Nov 17, 1887—Bernard Law Montgomery born in Kennington, London, England.

Jan 20, 1907—Enters Sandhurst Military Academy.

Sep 19, 1908—Commissioned a Second Lieutenant in the 1st Battalion the Royal Warwickshire Regiment.

1908-1913—Serves with 1st Battalion Royal Warwickshire Regiment in India.

Aug 26, 1914—Participates in Battle of Le Cateau.

Oct 13, 1914—During first battle of Ypres, Montgomery wounded at Meteren, evacuated to Britain, and awarded Distinguished Service Order.

Jan 28, 1916—Returns to France as Brigade Major, 104th Brigade.

Jan-Dec 1920—Student Staff College at Camberley.

Jul 1923—Publishes 49th Division "Tactical Notes" after review by B.H. Liddell Hart.

Jan 1926-Jan 1929—Assigned as an instructor at Camberley Staff College.

Jul 27, 1927—Marries Betty Carver.

Aug 18, 1928—Son David born.

Jul 10, 1930—Posted to 1st Battalion Royal Warwickshire Regiment as second in command.

Sep 1930—Publishes *Infantry Training Manual*.

Jan 1931-Jun 1934—Montgomery takes command of 1st Battalion Royal Warwickshire Regiment, Palestine, Egypt, and India.

Jun 1934-May 1937—Chief instructor at Quetta, India Staff College.

Aug 5, 1937-Oct 28, 1938—Commands the 9th Infantry Brigade in Portsmouth.

Oct 19, 1937—Betty Montgomery dies.

Oct 28, 1938-Aug 23, 1939—Commands the 8th Division in Palestine.

Aug 28, 1939—Takes command of 3rd Division in England.

Sep 29, 1939—3rd Division deploys to France.

May 30, 1940—Takes command of II Corps at Dunkirk.

Jun 1, 1940—Evacuated from Dunkirk.

Jun 6, 1940—Resumes command of 3rd Division.

Jul 11, 1940—Made a Companion of the Order of the Bath.

Jul 22, 1940-Apr 1, 1941– Promoted to Lieutenant General, commands V Corps.

Apr 1, 1941-Nov 17, 1941– Commands XII Corps.

Nov 17, 1941-Aug 7, 1942– Takes over Southeastern Command.

Aug 12, 1942—Arrives in Cairo, Egypt.

Aug 15, 1942—Officially takes command of the British Eighth Army.

Aug 19, 1942—Raid at Dieppe ends in disaster.

Aug 30-Sep 5, 1942—Battle of Alam Halfa.

Oct 23-Nov 5, 1942—Second Battle of Alamein.

Nov 8, 1942—Operation Torch launched, Allies land at Morocco and Algeria.

Nov 11, 1942—Made a Knight Grand Cross of the Order of the Bath.

Nov 13, 1942—Takes Tobruk.

Nov 20, 1942—Takes Benghazi.

Dec 25, 1942—Takes Sirte.

Jan 23, 1943—Takes Tripoli.

Mar 16-26, 1943—Battle of Mareth Line.

Jul 9-Aug 17, 1943—Campaign in Sicily.

Aug 10, 1943—Awarded the title of Chief Commander of the Legion of Merit of the United States.

Sep 3-Dec 31, 1943—Leads Eighth Army in Italy.

Dec 31, 1943—Departs British Eighth Army in Italy to take up his role in the planning the summer invasion of Europe in which he would command all land forces.

Jan 3, 1944—Ordered back to England to take command of British troops in the Allied Expeditionary Force.

Apr 7, 1944—Briefs senior leaders on the invasion of France, stating the city of Caen would be captured on the first day of it.

Jun 6, 1944—Lands 21st Army Group at Normandy for Operation Overlord.

Jun 20, 1944—Awarded the title of Grand Commander of the Order of King George I of Greece.

Jul 20, 1944—Takes Caen.

Sep 1, 1944—Promoted to the rank of Field Marshal.

Sep 4, 1944—Takes Antwerp, neglects to secure seaward approaches to the port.

17-Sep 25, 1944—Operation Market Garden fails to gain crossing of Lower Rhine.

2 Oct-Nov 8, 1944—Seizes seaward approaches to Port of Antwerp in Battle of the Scheldt.

Oct 31, 1944—Awarded the Virtuti Militari V Class of Poland.

9-Nov 27, 1944—Scheldt Estuary cleared of mines.

Nov 28, 1944—Opens Port of Antwerp as first Allied ship arrives.

Dec 16, 1944-Jan 25, 1945—German Ardennes Offensive.

Mar 24, 1945—Leads 21st Army Group over the Rhine.

May 3, 1945—Meets a German delegation on Luneberg Heath, offering the surrender of all their forces in northwestern Germany.

May 22, 1945—Designated commander of British occupation troops and member of the Allied Control Commission in Germany.

Jun 5, 1945—With Eisenhower, awarded the Order of Victory, the Soviet Union's highest award.

Aug 2, 1945—Awarded the Order of the Elephant of Denmark.

1946-1948—Serves as the Chief of the Imperial General Staff.

Jan 16, 1947—Awarded the Order of Suvorov 1st Class of the Soviet Union and the Grand Cross of the Order of the Dutch Lion of the Netherlands.

1958—Publishes memoirs.

Mar 24, 1976—Dies in Alton, Hampshire, England, United Kingdom.

APPENDIX 3:
COMPARATIVE OFFICER RANKS

ARMY

British Army	American Army	German Army
Field Marshal	General of the Army	Generalfeldmarschall
General	General	Generaloberst
Lieutenant General	Lieutenant General	General of Infantry, etc.
		. . .
Major General	Major General	Generalleutnant
Brigadier	Brigadier General	Generalmajor
Colonel	Colonel	Oberst
Lieutenant Colonel	Lieutenant Colonel	Oberstleutnant
Major	Major	Major
Captain	Captain	Hauptmann
Lieutenant	First Lieutenant	Oberleutnant
Second Lieutenant	Second Lieutenant	Leutnant

APPENDIX 4: COMPARATIVE COMMANDS

Army Group

British Army	American Army	German Army
Field Marshal/ General	General	Generalfeldmarschall

Army

General/Lieutenant General	General/ Lieutenant General	Generaloberst/ General of Infantry, etc. . . .

Corps

Lieutenant General	Lieutenant General/ Major General	General of Infantry, etc. . . .

Division

Major General	Major General	Generalleutnant

Brigade

Brigadier

Regiment

Colonel   Colonel   Oberst

Battalion

Lieutenant Colonel/ Major   Lieutenant Colonel/ Major   Oberstleutnant/ Major

Company

Captain Lieutenant/   Captain First Lieutenant/   Hauptmann Oberleutnant/

Platoon

Lieutenant/ Second Lieutenant   First Lieutenant/ Second Lieutenant   Oberleutnant/ Leutnant

APPENDIX 5:
MAPS

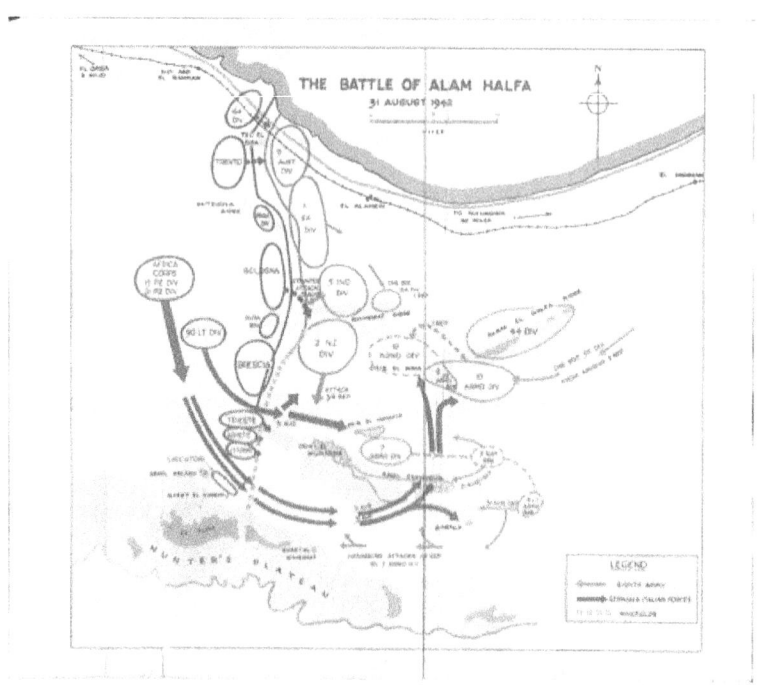

MAP 1. The Battle of Alam Halfa 30 August-5 September 1942, Montgomery's first Victory. From *El Alamein to the River Sangro* (1958) by Field Marshal Bernard Montgomery.

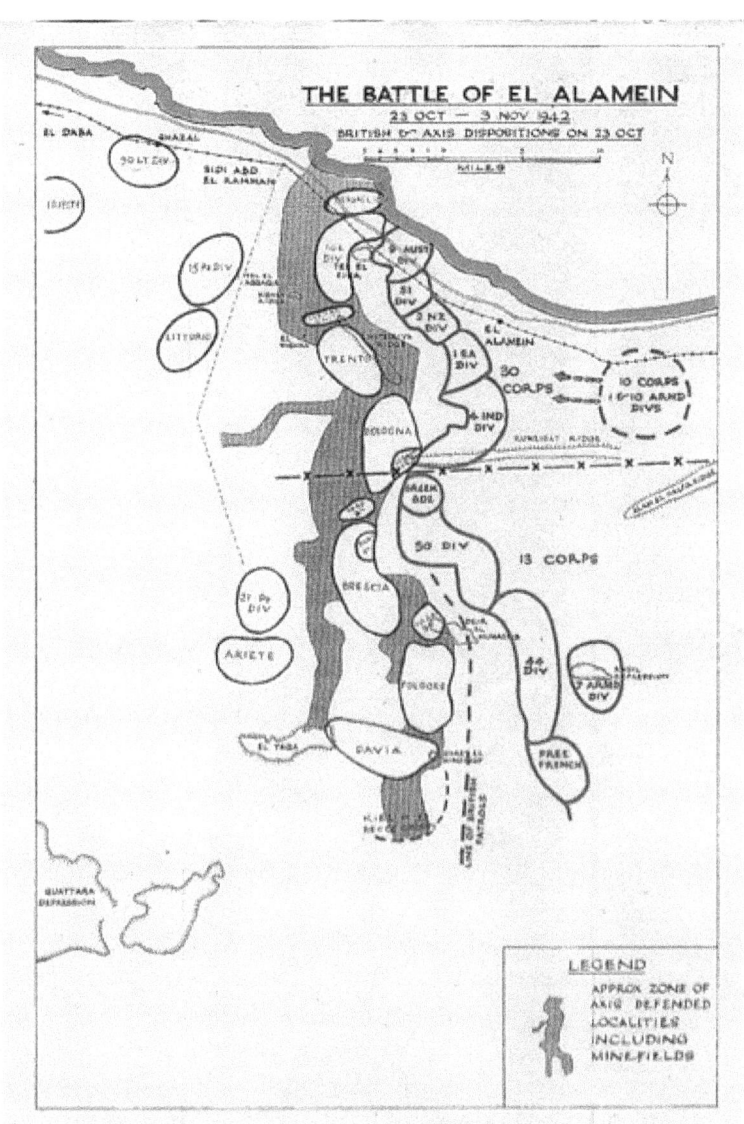

MAP 2. Second Battle of Alamein 23 Oct-Nov 11, 1942. From *El Alamein to the River Sangro* (1958) by Field Marshal Bernard Montgomery.

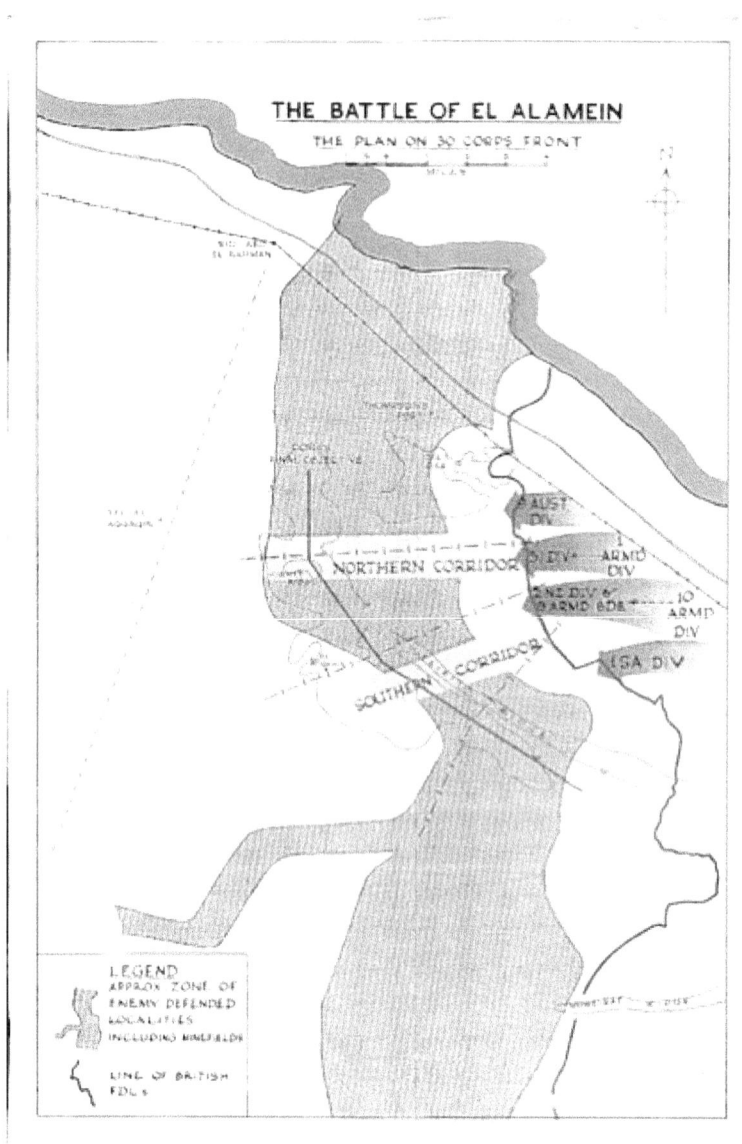

MAP 3. Second Battle of Alamein 23 Oct-Nov 11, 1942. From *El Alamein to the River Sangro* (1958) by Field Marshal Bernard Montgomery.

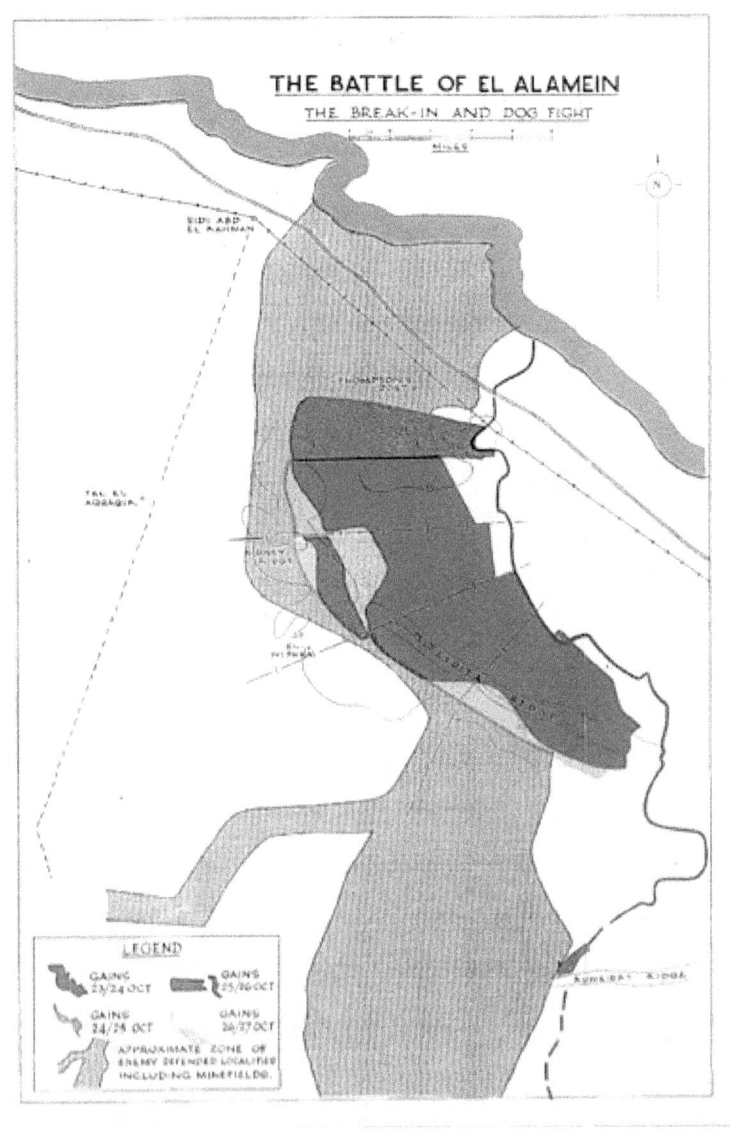

MAP 4. Second Battle of Alamein 23 Oct-Nov 11, 1942. From *El Alamein to the River Sangro* (1958) by Field Marshal Bernard Montgomery.

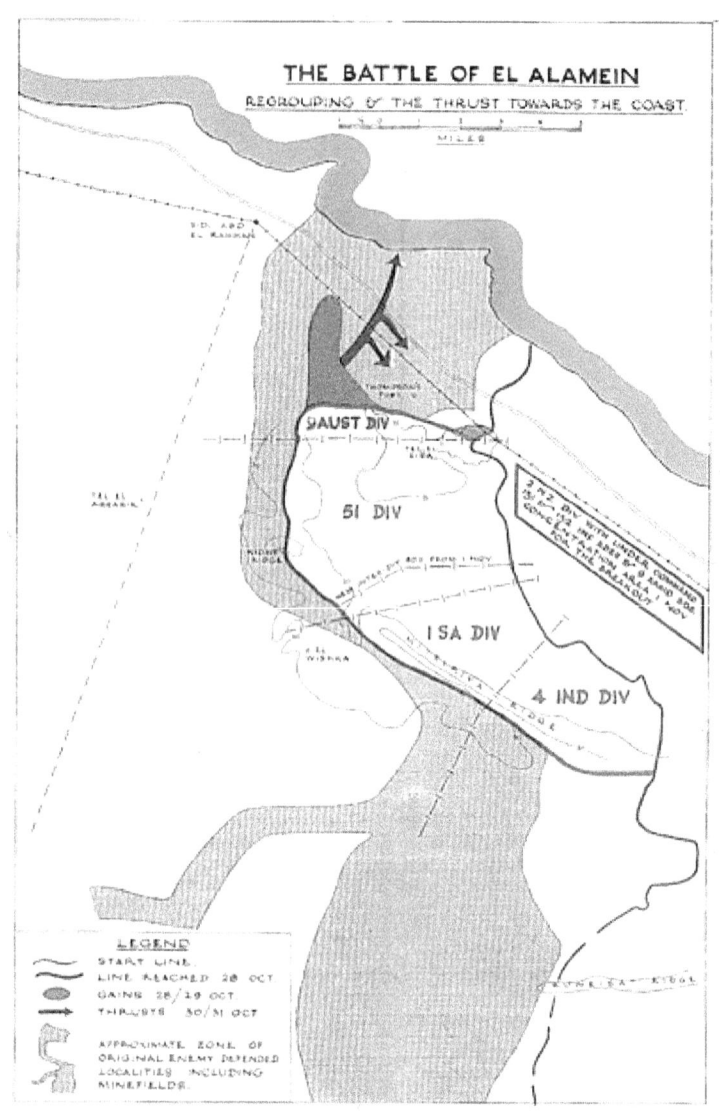

MAP 5. Second Battle of Alamein 23 Oct-Nov 11, 1942. Montgomery changes the plan. From *El Alamein to the River Sangro* (1958) by Field Marshal Bernard Montgomery.

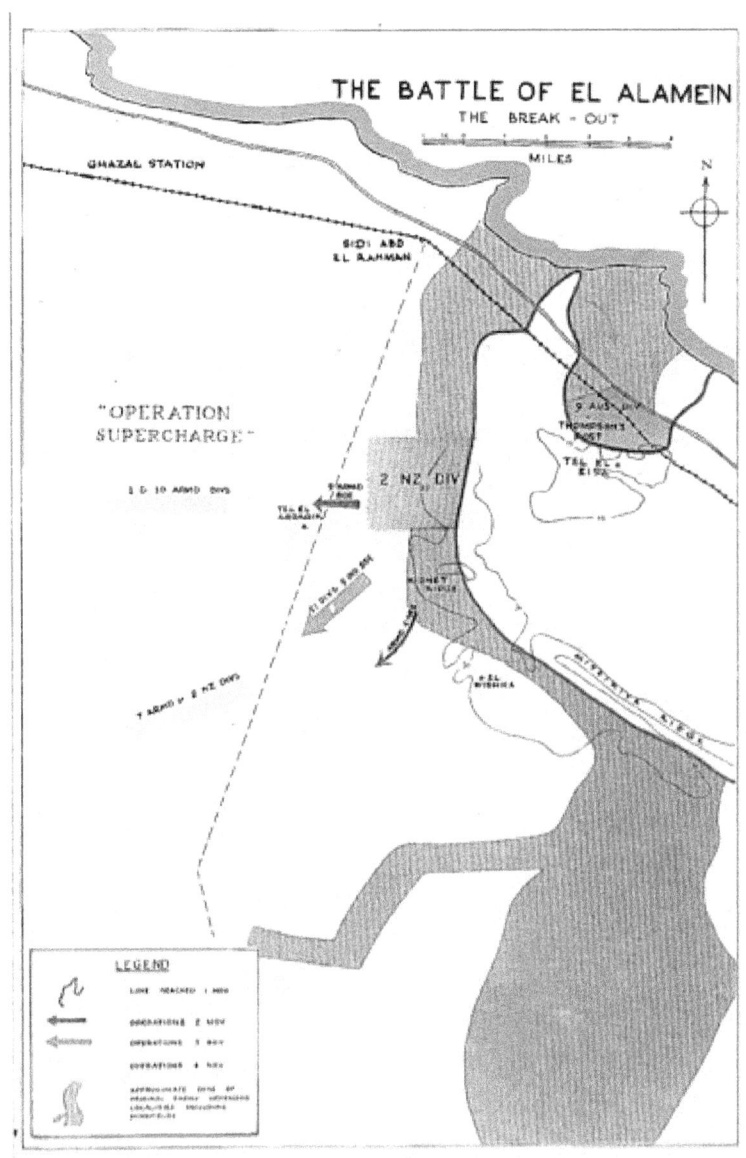

MAP 6. Second Battle of Alamein 23 Oct-Nov 11, 1942. Montgomery demonstrates flexibility by changing the plan once more. From *El Alamein to the River Sangro* (1958) by Field Marshal Bernard Montgomery.

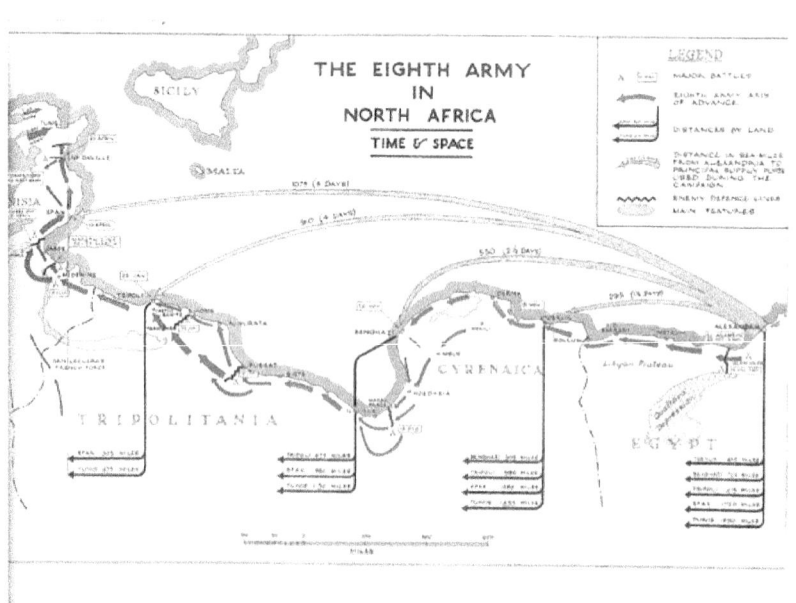

MAP The 7, Pursuit. From *El Alamein to the River Sangro* (1958) by Field Marshal Bernard Montgomery.

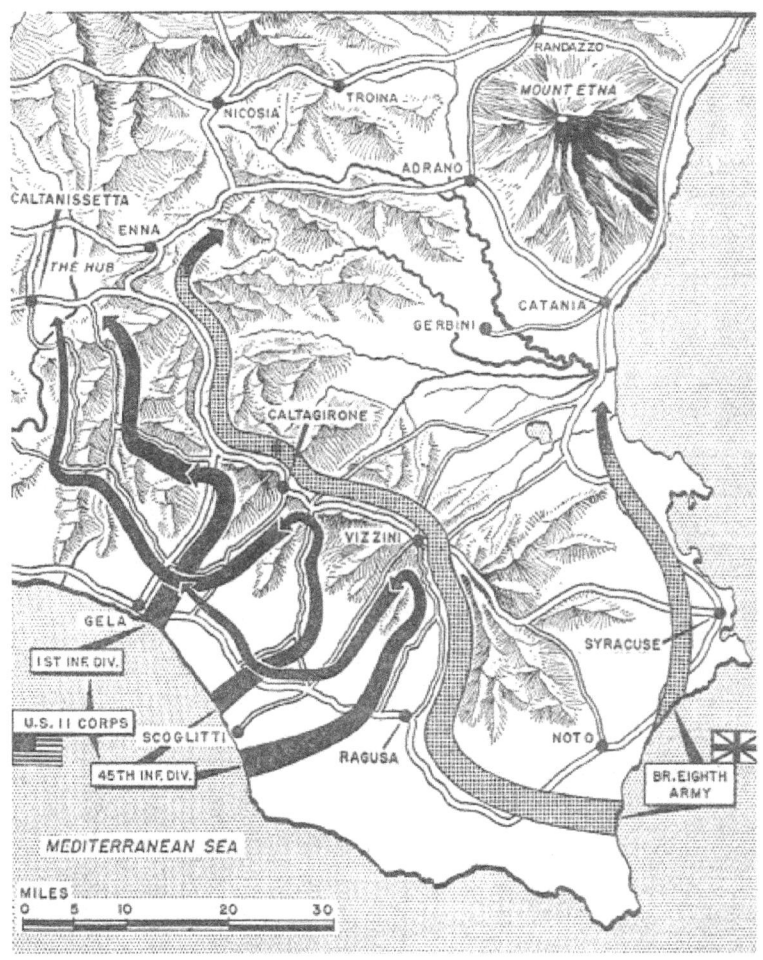

MAP 8. Montgomery takes High Way 124. From *A General's Life* (1983) by Omar Bradley.

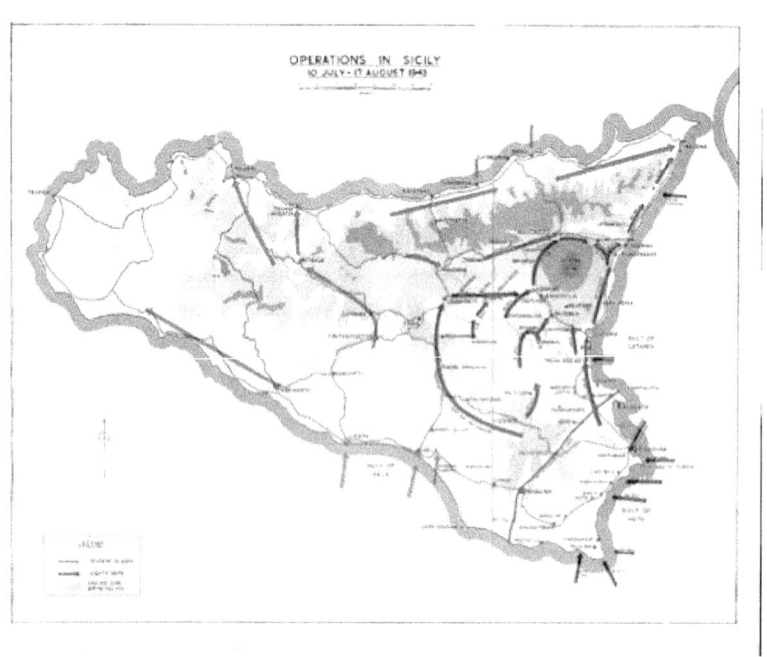

MAP 9. Sicily Operations 10 July—17 August 1943. From *El Alamein to the River Sangro* (1958) by Field Marshal Bernard Montgomery.

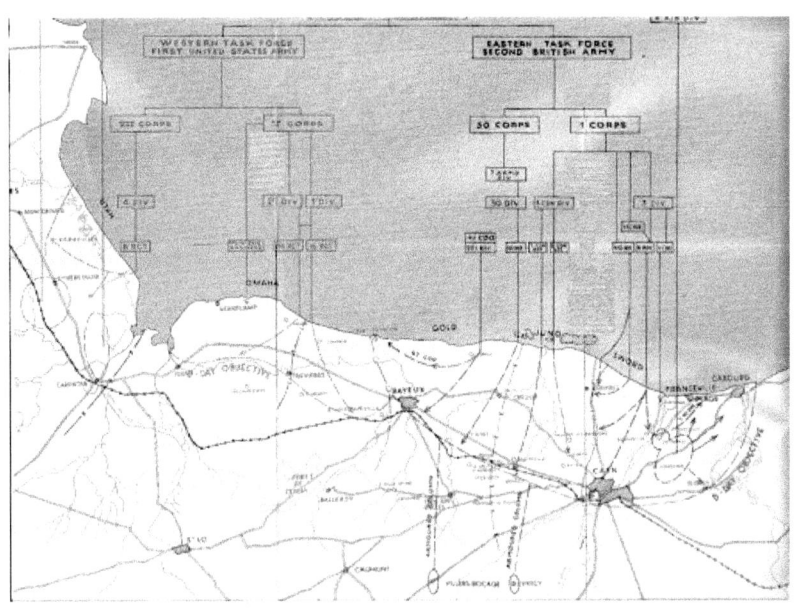

MAP 10. Allied landings on Normandy. Montgomery's graphics confirm Caen was a D-Day objective. From *Normandy to the Baltic* (1946) by Field Marshal Bernard Montgomery.

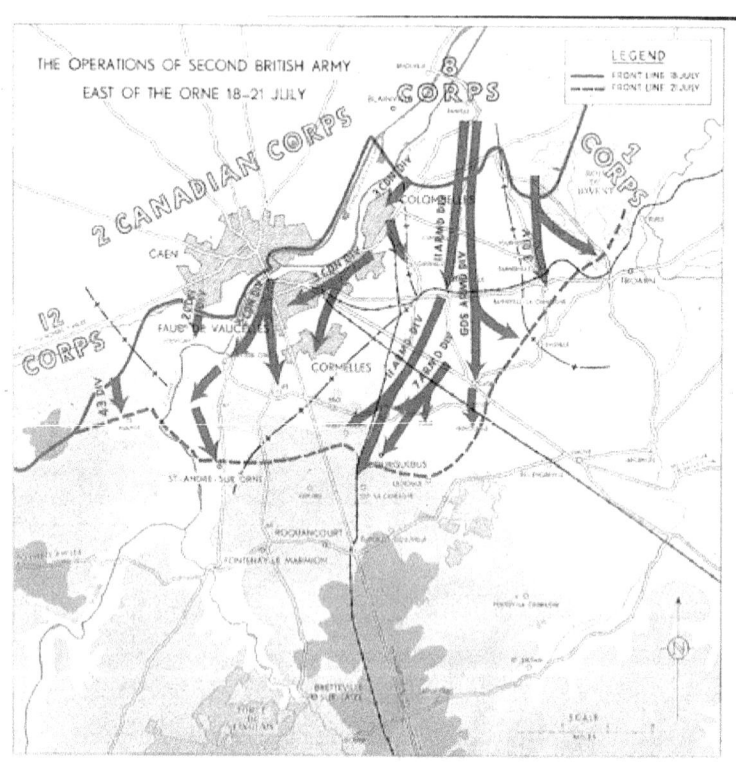

MAP 11. Operation Goodwood 18-20 July 1944. Breakout attempt fails. *From Normandy to the Baltic* (1946) by Field Marshal Bernard Montgomery.

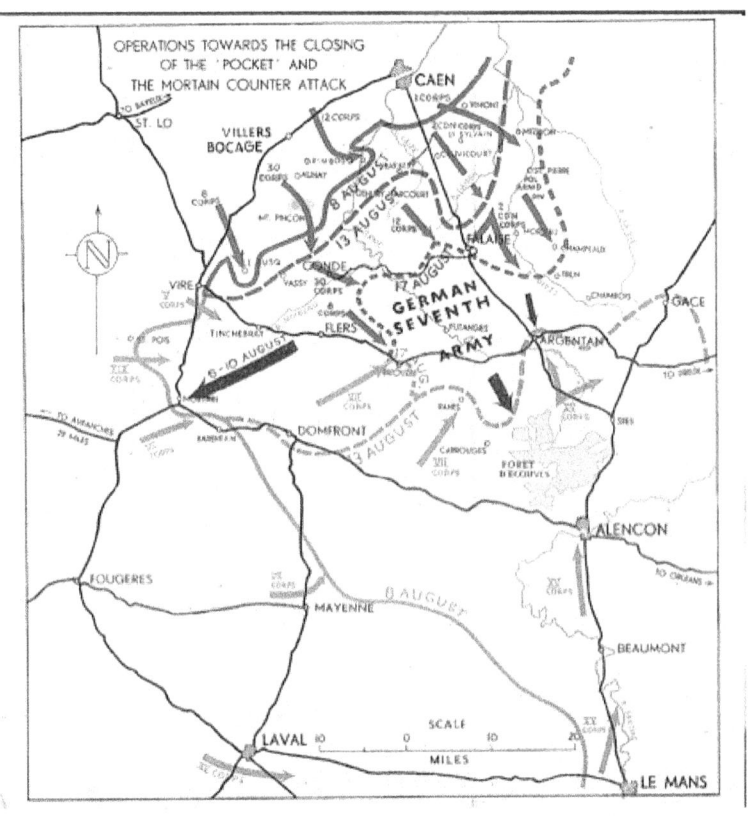

MAP 12. Initial plan to close the Falaise Gap From *El Alamein to the River Sangro* (1958) by Field Marshal Bernard Montgomery.

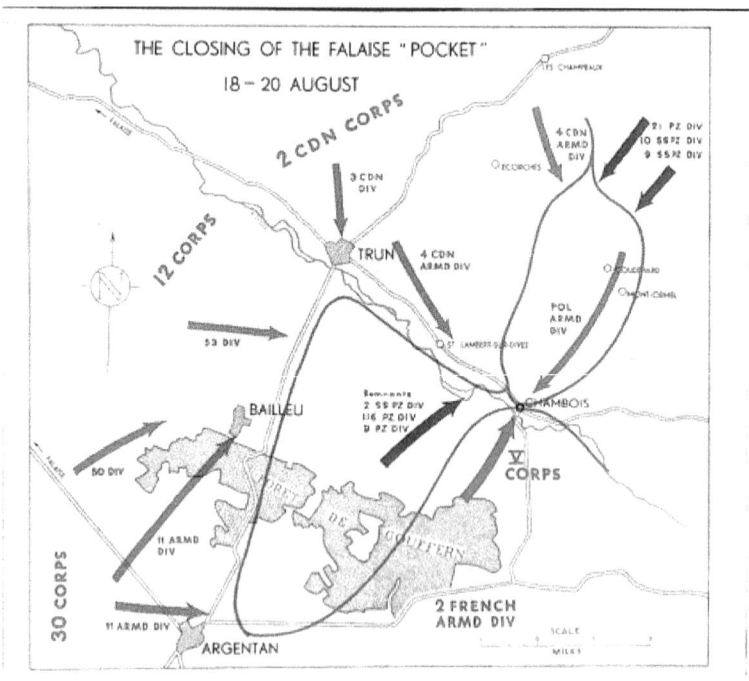

MAP 13. The Falaise Gap is closed at Chambois. From *El Alamein to the River Sangro* (1958) by Field Marshal Bernard Montgomery.

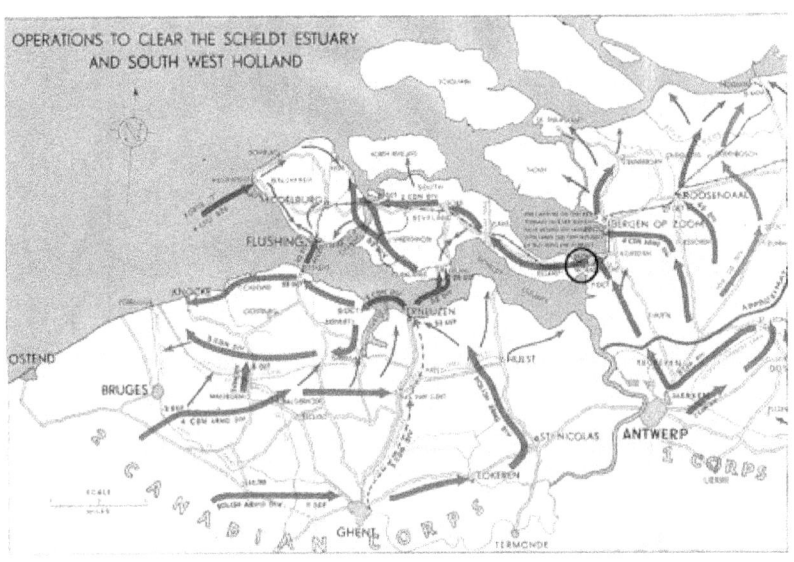

MAP 14. Clearing the Scheldt. If Montgomery's forces had seized the Key Terrain on 4 or Sep 5, 1944, by pushing on another 25 km, the Germans would have lost the opportunity to block the Scheldt. From *Normandy to the Baltic* (1946) by Field Marshal Bernard Montgomery.

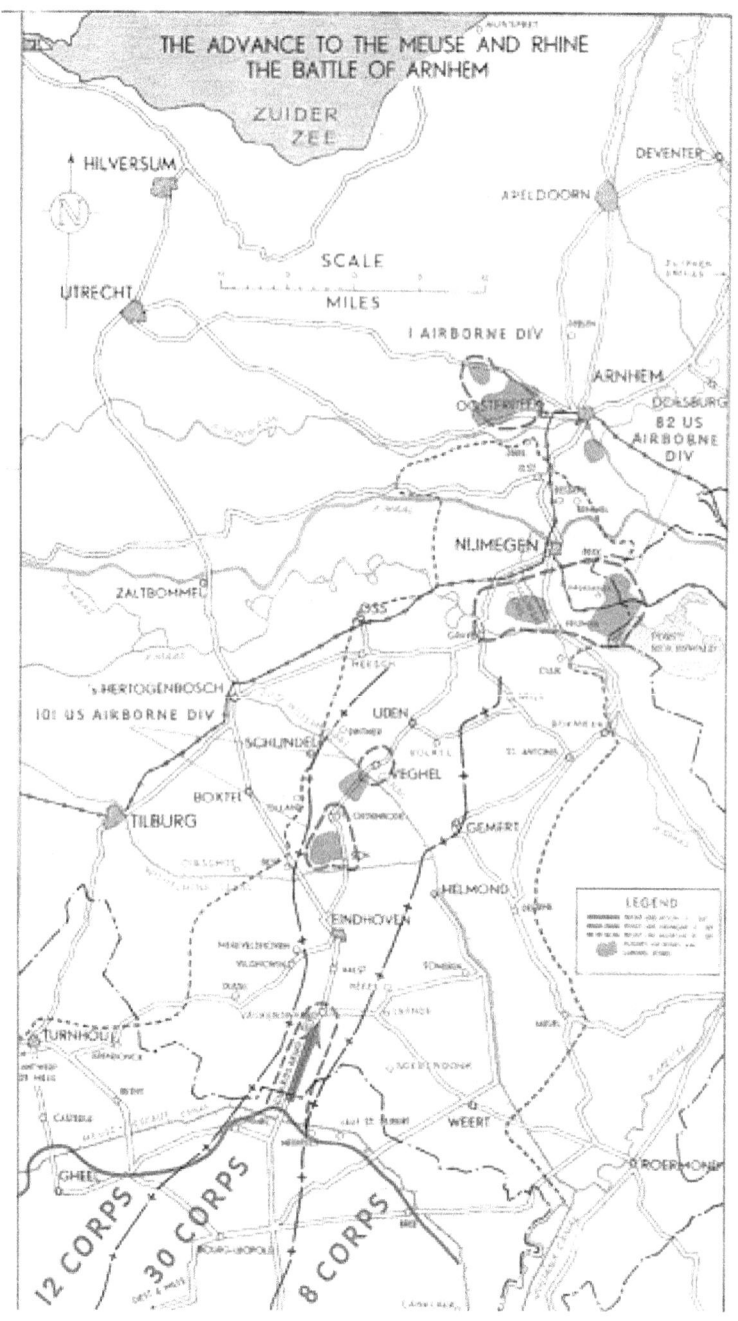

MAP 15. Operation Market Garden 17-Sep 25, 1944. From *Normandy to the Baltic* (1946) by Field Marshal Bernard Montgomery.

BIBLIOGRAPHY

Alanbrooke, Lord. *War Diaries 1939-1945*. Berkeley: University of California Press, 2001.

Alexander, Earl of Tunis. *Memoirs 1940-1945*. London: Cassel, 1962.

Allen, Peter. *One More River: The Rhine Crossings of 1945*. New York: Scribner's Sons, 1980.

Ambrose, Steven. *Eisenhower: Soldier and President*. New York: Simon and Schuster, 1990.

Anderson, J.K. *Military Theory and Practice in the Age of Xenophon*. Berkeley: University of

California Press, 1970.

Atkinson, Rick. *An Army at Dawn*. New York: Henry Holt, 2002.

_____. *The Guns at Last Light*. New York: Henry Holt, 2013.

Arnold, Michael. *Hollow Heroes*. Oxford: Casemate, 2015.

Atkinson, Rick. *The Day of Battle: The War in Sicily and Italy 1943-1944*. New York: Henry Holt, 2007.

Baldwin, Hanson. *Battles Lost and Won: Great Campaigns of World War II.* Old Saybrook, CT.:

Konecky and Konecky, 1966.

Barnett, Correlli. *The Desert Generals.* Bloomington, IN.: Indiana University Press, 1982.

Beale, Peter. *The Great Mistake: The Battle for Antwerp and the Breveland Peninsula,*

September 1944. Gloucestershire, UK: The History Press, 2004.

Beevor, Anthony. *D-Day The Battle for Normandy.* New York: Viking, 2009.

Bennett, Ralph. "Ultra and Some Command Decisions," *Journal of Contemporary History*, Vol. 16, No. 1, (Jan. 1981). Accessed December 13, 2015. http://www.jstor.org.ezproxy2.apus.edu/stable/pdf/260620.pdf?acceptTC=true.

_____. *Ultra in the West: The Normandy Campaign 1944-1945.* New York: Schribner's

Sons, 1979.

Blumenson, Martin. *Breakout and Pursuit.* Washington D.C.: Center of Military History United

States Army, 1984.

_____. "General Bradley's Decision at Argentan, 1944." In *Command Decisions*, edited by

Kent Greenfield, 303-319. New York: Harcourt, Brace and Company, 1959.

_____. *The Battle of the Generals.* New York: William Morrow, 1993.

_____. Ed., *The Patton Papers 1940-1945.* Boston: Houghton Mifflin, 1974.

Bradley, Omar. *A Generals Life.* New York: Simon and Schuster, 1983.

_____. *A Soldier's Story.* New York: Simon and Schuster, 1951.

Brooks, Stephen. Ed. *Montgomery and the Eighth Army: A Selection from the Diaries, Correspondence and other Papers of the Viscount Montgomery of Alamein, August 1942 to December 1943*. London: Army Records Society, 1991.

Butcher, Harry. *My Three Years with Eisenhower: The Personal Diary of Captain Harry C. Butcher, USNR, Naval Aide to General Eisenhower, 1942 to 1945.* New York: Simon and Schuster, 1946.

Carver, Michael. *El Alamein*. London: B.T. Batsford, 1963.

_____. "Montgomery." In *Churchill's Generals,* edited by John Keegan, 148–65. New

York: Grove Weidenfeld, 1991.

Chandler, Alfred. Ed. *The Papers of Dwight David Eisenhower, The War Years:* Vol.4

Baltimore: John Hopkins Press, 1970.

Churchill, Winston S. *Triumph and Tragedy*. Boston: Houghton Mifflin Company, 1953.

Clark, Mark. *Calculated Risk*. New York: Enigma Books, 2007.

Clausewitz, Carl von. *On War*. Princeton: Princeton University Press, 1976.

Clark, Lloyd. *Operation Epsom*. Gloucestershire, UK: Sutton Publishing, 2004.

Clifford, Alexander. *Three Against Rommel: The Campaigns of Wavell, Auchinleck and Alexander*. London: George G. Harrap and Company, 1943.

Cole, Hugh M. *The Ardennes: The Battle of the Bulge.* (Washington DC: Office of the Chief of Military History, 1965.

_____. *The Lorraine Campaign*. Washington, D.C.: Center of Military History, 1993.

Colley, David. *Decision at Strasbourg*. Annapolis, MD: Naval Institute Press, 2008.

Collins, J. Lawton. *Lightening Joe*. Baton Rouge: Louisiana State University Press, 1979.

Delaforce, Patrick. *Monty's Highlanders*. London: Chancellor Press, 2000.

D' Este, Carlo. *Bitter Victory: The Battle for Sicily, 1943*. New York: Harper Perennial, 2008.

_____. *Decision In Normandy*. New York: E.P. Dutton, 1994.

_____. Patton: *A Genius for War*. New York: Harper Collins, 1995.

De Guingand, Francis. *From Brass Hat to Bowler Hat*. London: Hamish Hamilton, 1979.

_____. *Generals at War*. London: Hodder and Stoughton, 1964.

_____. *Operation Victory*. London: Hodder and Stoughton, 1947.

Dupuy, Trevo. *Hitler's Last Gamble: The Battle of the Bulge, December 1944–January 1945*. New York: Harper Collins, 1994.

Dimbleby, Jonathan. *Destiny in the Desert: The Road to Alamein—The Battle that Turned the Tide* of *World War II*. New York: Pegasus Books, 2013.

Dixon, Dr. Norman. *On the Psychology of Military Incompetence*. London: Futura Publications, 1985.

Eisenhower, Dwight. *Crusade in Europe*. Garden City, NJ: Doubleday, 1948.

_____. *Eisenhower's Own Story of the War: The Complete Report of the Supreme Commander on the War in Europe From the Day of Invasion to the Day of Victory*. New York: ARCO Publishing, 1946.

Eisenhower, John S.D. *The Bitter Woods*. New York: G.P. Putnam's Sons, 1969.

Engle, Gerhard. *At the Heart of the Reich: The Secret Diary of Hitler's Army Adjutant*. Trans. Geoffrey Brooke. London: Greenhill Books, 2005.

Fraser, David. *And We Shall Shock Them: The British Army in the Second World War*. London: Book Club Associates, 1983.

Fuller, J.F.C. *Decisive Battles of the Western World and Their Influence Upon History*. Vol. 3. *From the American Civil War to the End of the Second World War*. London: Cassell and Company, 2001.

_____. *The Second World War 1939-1945*. New York: Da Capo Press, 1993.

Garland, Albert and Howard Smyth, *Sicily and the Surrender of Italy*. Washington D.C.: Office of the Chief of Military History United States Army, 1965.

Halder, Franz. *The Halder War Diary 1939-1942*. Edited by Charles Burdick and Hans-Adolf Jacobson. Novato, CA: Presidio, 1988.

Hamilton, Nigel. *Master of the Battlefield: Monty's War Years 1942-1944*. New York: McGraw-Hill, 1983.

_____. *Monty: Final Years of the Field Marshal 1944-1976*. New York: McGraw-Hill, 1986.

_____. *Monty The Battles of Field Marshal Bernard Montgomery*. New York: Random House, 1994.

_____. *Monty: The Making of a General 1887-1942*. New York: McGraw-Hill, 1981.

Hastings, Max. *Armageddon*. New York: Alfred A. Knopf, 2004.

_____. *Das Reich: The March of the 2nd SS Panzer Division Through France*. New York:

Holt, Rinehart and Winston, 1981.

_____. *Overlord: D-Day and the Battle for Normandy*. New York: Simon and Schuster, 1984.

Horne, Alistair, "In Defense of Montgomery," *In No End Save Victory: Perspectives on World War II*. Edited by Robert Crowley, 474-493. New York: Putnam's Sons, 2001.

Horne, Alistair, and David Montgomery. *The Lonely Leader: Monty 1944-45*. London: Macmillan, 1994.

Horrocks, Brian. *A Full Life*. London: Collins, 1960.

_____. *Corps Commander*. London: Magnum Books, 1977.

Keegan, John. *Six Armies in Normandy: From D-Day to the Liberation of Paris June 6th–August 25th, 1944*. New York: Viking Press, 1982.

_____. *The Second World War*. London: Penguin Books, 1989.

Kesselring, Albert. *The Memoirs of Field Marshal Kesselring*. London: Greenhill Books, 2007.

Lamb, Richard. *Montgomery in Europe 1943-1945*. New York: Franklin Watts, 1984.

Lewin, Ronald. *Montgomery as Military Commander*. London: B.T. Batsford, 1971.

Liddell Hart, B.H. *The Liddell Hart Memoirs 1895-1938*. Vol. 1. New York: G.P. Putnam's Sons, 1965.

_____. Ed. *The German Generals Talk*. New York: William Morrow, 1971.

_____. Ed. *The Rommel Papers*. New York: Harcourt, Brace and Company, 1953.

_____. *The Tanks: The History of the Royal Tank Regiment, 1939-1945*. Vol. 2. London: Cassell, 1959.

Luck, Hans von. *Panzer Commander: The Memoirs of Colonel Hans von Luck*. New York: Dell, 1989.

MacLeod, R. and Denis Kelly, eds., *Time Unguarded: The Ironside Diaries 1937-1940*. New York: David McKay, 1963.

Marshall, S.L.A. *Battle at Best*. New York: William Morrow and Company, 1963

Mason, David. *Breakout: Drive to the Seine*. New York: Ballantine Books, 1972.

McCormack. P.J. "Leadership: Proceedings of a Symposium Held at the Royal

Military Academy Sandhurst." *Sandhurst Occasional Papers No. 18*. Camberley, UK: Royal Military Academy Sandhurst, 2014.

Mellenthin, von F.W. *Panzer Battles: A Study of the Employment of Armor in the Second WorldWar*. Translated by H. Betzler. Old Saybrook, CT: Konecky and Konecky, 1956.

Milner, Marc. "Stopping the Panzers: Reassessing the Role of 3rd Canadian Infantry Division in Normandy, 7-10 June 1944," *The Journal of Military History*, (April 2010), 491-522. Accessed December 15, 2015. http://search.proquest.com.ezproxy2.apus.edu/docview/195636835?pq-origsite=summon&accountid=8289.

Montgomery, Viscount of Alamein. *A History of Warfare*. New York: William Morrow, 1983.

_____. *El Alamein to the River Sangro*. London: Hutchinson, 1958.

_____. *Memoirs, Montgomery of Alamein*. Cleveland: World Publishing Company, 1958.

_____. *Normandy to the Baltic*. London: Hutchinson and Company, 1946.

_____. *The Path to Leadership*. London: Collins, 1961.

Morison, Samuel. *History of United States Naval Operations in World War II*. Vol. 9, *Sicily—Salerno—Anzio January 1943—June 1944*. Chicago: University of Illinois Press, 2002.

Mussolini, Benito. *Mussolini: Memoirs 1942-1943*. London: George Weidenfeld and Nicolson, 1949.

Nicolson, Nigel. *Alex*. London: Weidenfeld and Nicolson, 1973.

Neillands, Robin, *The Battle for the Rhine: The Battle for the Budge and the ArdennesCampaign, 1944*. New York: The Overlook Press, 2005.

Overy, Richard. *Why the Allies Won*. New York: Norton and Company, 1995.

Pauchau, Guy and Pierre Masfrand. *Oradour sur Glane, A Vision of Horror*. Oradour-sur-Glane, FR: Association Nationale Des Familles Des Martyers

D'Oradour-sur-Glane, 2003.

Playfair, I.S.O. et al. *The Destruction of the Axis Forces in Africa*. Vol. 4, *The Mediterranean and Middle East*. Uckfield, UK: 2009.

Pogue, Forrest. *George C. Marshall, Organizer of Victory 1943-1945*. New York: Viking Press, 1973.

Robertson, Terence. *Dieppe: The Shame and the Glory*. Boston: Little, Brown and Company, 1962.

Royal Military Academy. "Sandhurst Guide to Developing Leaders." Camberley UK.: Royal Military Academy Sandhurst, 2012.

Royle, Trevor. *Montgomery: Lessons in Leadership from the Soldier's General*. New York: Palgrave Macmillan, 2010.

Ruge, Friedrich. *Rommel in Normandy*. San Rafael, CA: Presidio Press, 1979.

Ryan, Cornelius. *A Bridge Too Far*. New York: Simon and Schuster, 1974.

Saunders, Tim. *Operation Plunder and Varsity: The British and Canadian Rhine Crossing*. Barnsley, UK: Pen and Sword, 2006.

Semmens, Steven. *Decision Making in Alliance Warfare: Operation Market Garden—A Case Study*. Carlisle Barracks, PA.: U.S. Army War College, 2001.

Strawson, John. *The Italian Campaign*. London: Martin Secker and Warbug, 1987.

Sylvan, Major William and Captain Francis Smith. *Normandy to Victory: The War Diary of General Courtney Hodges and the First U.S. Army*. Lexington: University Press of Kentucky, 2008.

Toland, John. Battle, *The Story of the Bulge*. New York: Random House, 1959.

Tout, Ken. *A Fine Night for Tanks: The Road to Falaise*, Gloucestershire, UK: Sutton Publishing, 2002.

Trythall, Anthony. *Boney Fuller, Soldier, Strategist, and Writer 1878-1966*. New Brunswick, NJ: Rutgers University Press, 1977.

Wade, David. "Battle of Monmouth," *Military History*, (June 1998), Accessed February 25, 2016. http://www.historynet.com/battle-of-monmouth.htm.

Warlimont, Walter. *Inside Hitler's Headquarters 1939-1945*. Translated by R.H. Barry. Novato, CA: Presidio, 1964.

Warner, Philip. "Auchinleck." In *Churchill's Generals,* edited by John Keegan, 130–47. New York: Grove Weidenfeld, 1991.

Wasserstein, Bernard. *Barbarism and Civilization: A History of Europe In Our Time*. Oxford: Oxford University Press, 2007.

Watson, Bruce. *Exit Rommel: The Tunisian Campaign, 1942–4*. Mechanicsburg, PA: Stackpole, 2006.

Watts, Martin, "Operation Market Garden: Strategic Masterstroke or Battle of Egos?" *The Journal of the Historical Association*. Vol. 98, (April 2013), 191-201. Accessed December 12, 2015. http://yw6vq3kb9d.search.serialssolutions.com/?ctx_ver=Z39.88-2004&ctx_enc=info%3Aofi%2Fenc%3AUTF-8&rfr_id=info:sid/summon.

Weigley, Russell. *Eisenhower's Lieutenants, The Campaign of France and Germany 1944-1945*. Bloomington: Indiana University Press, 1981.

Wilmot, Chester. *The Struggle for Europe*. Old Saybrook, CT.: Konecky and Konecky, 1952.

Williams, Jeffery. *The Long Left Flank: The Hard Fought Way to the Reich 1944-1945*. Barnsley, UK: Pen and Sword, 1988.

Winterbotham, F.W. *The Ultra Secret*. NY: Harper and Row, 1974.

Yeide, Harry and Mark Stout. *First to the Rhine, The 6th Army Group in World War II*. St. Paul, MN: Zenith, 2007.

Zabecki, David. *Germany at War: 400 Years of Military History*. Santa Barbara: ABC-CLIO, 2014.

Zuehlke, Mark. *Terrible Victory: First Canadian Army and the Scheldt Estuary Campaign*. Vancouver: Douglas and McIntyre Ltd., 2007.

ACKNOWLEDGMENTS

I would like to thank all the great folks at the Ramstein Airbase, Germany Library who provided a haven where I could focus on the matter at hand. I also wish to thank Colonel Tim Whalen and Lieutenant Colonel Dan Meyers for proofreading the manuscript.

Lightning Source UK Ltd.
Milton Keynes UK
UKHW011332081220
374768UK00001B/43